FROM BANKRUPT TO MILLIONAIRE IN FOUR YEARS

From Bankrupt to Millionaire in Four Years

with manifestation, gut feeling and inspired action

METTE HÅ

Enlightened pages publishing

Contents

DISCLAIMER

The information in this book is intended for educational and entertainment purposes only. This book does not intend to substitute professional legal, medical, psychological, accounting, or financial advice. The author and publisher are not offering professional service advice. Additionally, this book does not serve as the basis for any financial or business decisions. If you need expert advice, you should seek the service of a professional. The author and publisher assume no responsibility for your actions and specifically disclaim responsibility for any liability, loss, risk, or any physical, psychological, emotional, financial, or commercial damage, personal or otherwise, which is incurred as a consequence, directly or indirectly of the use and application of any of the content in this book. The author and publisher make no warranty, representation, or guarantees about the information's accuracy or completeness.

Introduction - Was I brave? Yes, I was brave as fuck.

Was it shaky? Yes, it was shaky as fuck. Was I scared? Very. Did I do it anyway? Yes, I did.

Does that mean I understood the road ahead and knew what was coming? Not at all. Did I have self-doubt? Absolutely!

I will tell you that trusting the universe gives me a backbone of courage. The law of attraction, the law of purpose, and the law of compensation build a solid ground for my trust. Combined, they have taught me the most essential tools. When I set my goals, release the "how" to the universe, and start taking dedicated actions in the direction I want to go, my goal will magically manifest into reality.

As a child, I always looked at the big houses by the ocean and wondered how people could afford them. What would I have to do to get there?

Looking back, the road to getting the house with the perfect view wasn't that interesting. The story actually begins when I left the perfect house.

Not only did I leave the house, but I also left behind the man, the job, the platinum credit card, and all of my success values. In this book, I will tell you how I went from bankruptcy to becoming a millionaire and share all the tools I used to get there.

If you have lost your compass or financial self-esteem, I will guide you to your own growth experience, manifesting luxury and wealth so you, too, can feel the same financial freedom and abundance I have. This book focuses on financial freedom, but you will be guided on using the tools in other areas of your life.

Take what resonates with you and let go of the rest.

Chapter One

The feeling of hitting rock bottom

The guilt and blame I put upon myself for failing at my marriage and leaving my partner of 17 years was mixed with the feeling of excitement of following my dream.

When two people marry, they promise to support and protect each other in good and bad times. I had abandoned that security in exchange for the freedom to shape my future according to my terms.

I had a dream of opening a health and wellness center. A place where people could enjoy good, healthy, clean food, go for yoga, or get a spa treatment. I started looking around and asking questions. Was it possible to create such a place?

I wrote down what I saw in my vision, how I wanted people to feel and what kind of people would go there. A memory appeared in my mind that a political acquaintance also had a passion for clean food. I had met here a couple of times before when we were fighting for the kids' rights to get healthy food in school. We were not in the same political party, but that didn't matter to me since the end goal was the same.

I gave her a call to ask more about her background, education, and knowledge of nutrition. One thing led to the other and Magically, it turned out that she shared the same dream, as me. We decided to build this place together. We sat down, drew out a plan of what was important for each of us, and then started to act on it with inspiration and intention. Within two months, we had the third partner onboard and chose a location—the three of us were different types of people, but perfectly complimented each other.

The whole creation process was like one big showcase from the universe demonstrating what you can accomplish when your intentions are true and honest and come straight from the heart.

There were so many examples of how things magically worked out. I use the word magic, not randomly, because I genuinely believe in the magic of creation. One example that stands out is a visit by the health inspector. He wasn't supposed to come for another two months but called us because he was in the neighborhood. He was curious since we were the buzz of the town, so he just wanted to see the location and how we were coming along with our health and wellness center.

His visit was both good and bad for us. We were lucky he stopped by because he saw we were missing a drain in the middle of the kitchen. If he had come two months later, it would have cost us a fortune to correct. But it wasn't good because it was Friday and a quarter to four. You know the feeling when you think, "How the heck am I going to solve this"?

We had no bad luck; we only had good luck. As the health inspector stopped by, the boss of the plumber company also showed up. He had forgotten some tools from the day before. We stopped him and told him what was going on. He was in a good mood and said he would help us out. He thought he had all the parts necessary to fix the drain in his car and called another worker just across the street.

We called the entrepreneur who owned the building and asked if he would pay for this extra work, which he magically agreed to. Everyone did more than what was required of them, and fifteen minutes later, equipment, materials, and labor were all in place, and we got a newly molded hole in the ground. It felt like the stars had aligned, and everything fell into perfect harmony. It was as if the universe had conspired to make it happen precisely how it was meant to happen. It was magical!

The whole process up until the opening day was like that. Everything fell so easily into place. There is no doubt that opening this space was the right thing for me to do at that time. I am immensely proud of our vision. It was the first place in town that served gluten-free, soy-free, lactose-free, and sugar-free clean food. It was truly a health and wellness center. It was a combined space for chiropractors, masseuses, osteopaths, food specialists, healers, and other professionals who offered treatments like facials, EPL, and facial injections. There was even a huge yoga studio, café, hairdresser, and a shop. It was a space to relax and reflect and simply a space to be allowed to be just as you were, without any demand.

Coming from an industrial background, I used to kid that there was no goal for turnover time of our customers. They were allowed to sit as long as they needed without having to purchase anything. For me, not having turnover demands signaled freedom and compassion.

Unfortunately, after our launch, reality struck. Even if our sales were good, we almost immediately started to struggle internally amongst ourselves. For instance, when we were in the planning stage of our project, we had a shared vision that we would meditate before our weekly meetings. What weekly meetings? After our launch, we never once had a weekly meeting. One of us wanted to work in the morning, another preferred to work in the evening, and I preferred to work as much as possible one week and fewer hours the following week when I had my kids. There was never a good time to evaluate and plan our business together.

Our goal had always been to create and open this space. Of course, we knew what turnover would make the bank happy, but we never set new goals for ourselves. Hence, we started to drift in different directions, and after a couple of months, it became clear that the energy between us had shifted. The positive spirit we all had initially doing this project together suddenly shifted to a more negative one. All of our good intentions had sadly vanished. We had such low-level discussions, leaving me feeling alone, ashamed, lost, and stupid. At this point, I hit rock bottom and felt like a total failure.

I knew I needed help, so I asked a good friend for legal and emotional advice. Thankfully, I got myself out of that partnership with some of my dignity still in one piece. As a result, we split the company into two pieces. In our agreement, I was fortunate to keep the company's name and the actual shell of the company. Unfortunately, I also agreed to keep some of the contracts. At the same time, the other partners got the name of the store, assets, and debt. Keeping some contracts would cost me a fortune for many years to come but keeping the company name and registration would allow me to eventually start making workshops, having talks, and creating a calendar.

I had put all of my savings into building the company. Because of this split, my finances were gutted. I was at zero. I had no income or assets except the roof over my head, and the bills kept piling up. I really was at rock bottom. I had lost my compass and felt so empty and numb.

It even reached the point that every time I went out to empty the mailbox and found a new bill, I felt sick to my stomach, and it would turn. I had never felt anxiety before, but now I knew what it was like.

I didn't tell anyone what was happening except for that one friend because I was so ashamed. I thought I would fall deeper if I told anyone. I was only trying to survive.

By not telling others about my situation, I could hold on to some of the dignity I had not yet lost.

We get confused and drained when we are steering away from our path. The universe tells us in a very physical way that we are going in the wrong direction. All the energy had left me, and it felt like I was surrounded by this gray gum-like substance. Like a bubble surrounding me and making it hard to hear and move around. My steps were heavy and the sad feelings dragged me further down. I had fallen so hard that it was challenging to get up. The gray mass of despair just stuck to my body. It held a tight and firm grip on my entire being. I was at my lowest.

Of course, it would be nice to blame the other partners, but I just blamed myself and wondered where it all went wrong. I screamed at the universe so many times, wondering why it let me down when the path forward had been so clear to me. There was never a doubt in my mind that I shouldn't have gone down that road, and there still isn't. Today, I can appreciate all the lessons I have learned, but at the time, I just got numb because

I had lost my compass. I didn't even know how I would get through the next day or even the next hour. The road ahead of me was foggy and unsure. If I didn't take action and stayed in the gray zone, I would lose my house.

You don't have to hit rock bottom or be completely broke, like I was, to feel like you have lost your compass. It can happen as a result of everyday life. If you are surrounded by unsupportive people or have an uninspiring job, it is easy to get lost. The feeling can also come upon you in a more subtle way. You might enjoy your job, your kids, your activities, or whatever else you have going on in your life. You might want all that and still add more activities to your daily life, suddenly feeling like a hamster in the famous wheel. All these activities cause stress that, in turn, will create numbness and blind your vision. It will suck the glow out of your spirit and make you feel empty. I can totally relate to that.

In situations like this, it's normal to start searching for signs. You might spend hours a day on your phone trying to find the right enlightened person to follow—a person who will inspire you and guide you in the right direction. It is possible to find inspiration and guidance in the outer world, like this book. But let me tell you a secret. The best person to guide you is yourself. You are the one who holds all the solutions inside of you. You might not believe me, but it is true. You are an incredibly powerful force, and you are able to co-create your life together with the universe. I believe in you, and so does your spirit team. We are all here to help you.

One purpose of the book is to shift your focus from who you were yesterday, with the beliefs you had yesterday, into the person you are today, with the beliefs of who you can become tomorrow by being it today. By believing it today.

I will give you what you need to unlock your own potential, find your compass, and manifest wealth into your life. I will help you find and trust your gut feeling and find the essence of your being or your Geist, as I like to call it. I compare the Geist to a burning flame within us. It is our life force. I will share all of the small steps that collectively have taken me from rock bottom, seconds away from bankruptcy, to the happy millionaire I am today. I will help you define your inspired actions and draw more of the good stuff toward you. Let's do this together; let's go!

♥

Chapter Two

Small steps, enormous progress

I don't know about you, but many times in my life, I have set big goals for New Year's, and the day after, I knew this goal would never happen. For instance, we have this swim run where I live. Twice, I have attended this event as a volunteer resource with the Swedish Search and Rescue team.

Each time, I said that I wanted to participate in the actual run next year. Which, of course, never happened. Not because the goal was too big but because I could not see how I should get started. The hurdle to take the first step with the training was too big. I wished someone would take me by my hand, lead me through the exercise program, force me to keep my word and hold me accountable. I needed someone who guided me on how to prepare for the race step by step, from start to finish. This is what I will do for you in this book. I will hold your hand and guide you through your own growth by sharing what has worked for me and how you can adapt it to work for you.

After hitting rock bottom, creating my wealth was a process. I had to use small and simple steps not to be overwhelmed. Small steps are easier to accomplish. In this book, you will see how the small steps collectively add up to big progress.

When doing the steps, it is essential that you congratulate yourself for what you have done. So far, you can congratulate yourself on buying this book and being willing to look at ways to grow. Congratulations to you.

When we congratulate ourselves for completing steps, the brain creates new receptors and releases dopamine. The brain tells us to do more because it feels good. So, let's get that dopamine kicking. Congratulations on being right here, right now. Congratulations on taking active steps forward.

When you become aware, thankful, and proud of the steps you have taken, the brain starts to make new patterns, which is good for you. The dopamine and these new patterns will encourage you to continue taking other small steps.

Once you start to see some results, that, too, will teach your brain that these are good steps to follow. The brain will ensure you that you can do it. You can create wealth for yourself.

One of my favorite feelings is when the universe delivers something I have affirmed. When you see that starting to happen for you, it will trigger the dopamine in your brain and encourage you to do these exercises more often. It is science, and it works.

Like my friend Jenny said:

- 'Last week, I literally screamed at the universe, saying: "Goddamned, I AM ready to receive".'

The next day, she received four towels of really high quality from a lottery she had entered. My friend is into interior design and was very happy to win. The universe gave her proof, and that encouraged her to keep affirmation practice going.

You will find that the different exercises and routines I share throughout the book can be divided into three different categories:

1.   5-10-minute exercises you will only do once while reading this book and never again. You only need to do this once because that is enough to lift your energy and knowledge to a new plateau. You will find that you have peeled off a layer or two and shredded some old beliefs about what is possible for you. You will find that you have become a new, better version of yourself that can never be

reversed; therefore, you never need to do the exercise again.

2.   5-10-minute exercises that will last a couple of days because of the process. The different exercises have different purposes. Ultimately, the goal is to get you into the space of creating abundance and feeling worthy of receiving it so you can enjoy what you have created.

3.   Routines that will stick with you for the rest of your life because you see results immediately and enjoy the process of continuously evolving.

It is possible to create and receive without enjoying what you are getting. The worst case would be when you cannot keep what you have created just because you do not think you are worthy of it. For a long time, that was the case for me. I would self-sabotage because I didn't know I was worthy. In the fourth chapter, I will discuss how guilt, embarrassment, and shame are connected to the feeling of worthiness, but first, let's talk about illusions, what it is, and why I like the word so much.

♥

Chapter Three

Illusions

The only thing that is real is the present moment. Everything else is a memory with a perception of what happened in that moment. That perception is often, in spirituality, called an illusion. It is our perception of ourselves, the world around us, or happenings from the past.

An illusion is our perception of what has happened. Not the actual happenings. We could call an illusion for a story because it is something we make up. It is the brain's way of sorting out and archiving what happened at that exact moment that just passed.

The brain is amazing at making up stuff; it will do what it can to interpret information in a way that confirms what you already believe to be true. The brain will adjust its beliefs based on context, new information, and experience and therefore you can't really trust your memories.

Anyway, what do we really know to be true? Only you can tell me what is true for you. Therefore, your memory can look different from mine even if we were at the same place at the same time. It is common for siblings to have different memories of past experiences because of their age difference and their perception of their own selfish places of reference. A memory is our story about what happened in the past. Sometimes we even change it a little depending on who we tell the story to. Sometimes someone else has told us a story so many times that we believe it to be true.

My parents divorced when I was two. Throughout my upbringing, my mom and I talked from time to time about my parent's divorce. It was a subject that she didn't like to talk about. She would say stuff like, "It was too much party", "Your dad was out drinking with his friends a lot," or "You know me when things aren't fun, I take myself out of the situation". She always implied that my dad had been the problem, but that never rang true to me. In my world, she was the one who partied, not him.

When I visited my dad, we would always have a re-laxed and heartfelt social interaction—nothing like what my mom had described. When I would ask my dad why he had moved away to Saudi Arabia for a couple of years after their divorce he would be relaxed about it. Talking about the beginnings of the eighties and all the money that you could make in the building industry when Saudi

Arabia was a free country. He never said one bad word about my mom.

I never questioned any of it, but in my stomach, it didn't make sense. After my mom died, my sister and I would share memories and different perspectives of our upbringing. She would tell me how our dad would call us, but my mom wouldn't let him speak to us.

One time my dad had driven across the country to my mom's new house and knocked on the door, but she refused to let him in. I repeat, she just would not let him in. She didn't want him to see us. The following weeks, when it was his weekend to have us, she would bring us to other places and not be home when he arrived. He had no opportunity to be with us without involving the police. So he left.

I am too little to remember this, I only have fractions of conversations and images that pop up once in a while, so as a child I listened to my mom's version, but as I said, it never rang true to me.

My illusion could have been one of hatred toward him for not being there when I was little, but I trusted my gut and kept my thoughts of him high. Our illusions are created by our thoughts and beliefs, and thereby shape our reality, so If I had believed her interpretation of their separation, that would have created a different reality for me.

You never really know what stories people carry, or why they act the way they do, but remember that it really has something to do with you. You are only a mirror of their belief system.

I use the word illusion a lot, both when talking about my own life and also with people who ask for guidance. I like to question our perception, what we know to be true because I so often find that what is valid for one person is not true for the other. Like the clichés frais, "The more I study, the more I know that I don't know." These are tied to illusion because it explains so well that when you learn something new, first of all, you can never go back to not knowing, and second, with the new knowledge, a whole new world opens up.

It takes practice to change perspective. One way is to look at the story we make every day; how we look at the day we had when we go to bed. In the early 2000s, Oprah introduced the practice of gratitude journals. It is a practice where you end each day by saying thanks for at least three things that happened that day. For me, it was the first time I heard about it, but I have continued to do this practice on and off during my whole adult life.

When I was at my lowest, this was one of the practices I started doing on a more regular basis, every day. I make a conscious effort to identify at least three positive things to be grateful for, before going to sleep. Sometimes it is the simplest things like being thankful for the ability to breathe, walk, and talk. Other times, I have had truly connected moments throughout the day.

I will come back to this practice later in the book but for now, the most important part is for you to understand that my focus on the positive events, helps me make my illusions positive when going to sleep.

The next day when I wake up, I do a morning meditation, and then I record two messages to my friend Catarina.

The first message is about everything that I was grateful for yesterday. By starting the day today with repeating what I was grateful for, I create the emotion again and charge my body with new energy.

The second message I send her, is me explaining why today is going to be a magical day. I tell her where energy will flow, and what results I expect from that energy. She does the same with me. When her messages reach me first, I have a habit of recording mine without listening to hers, because I want my gut feeling and my energy to decide my day, not her message.

I will admit, that sometimes I am surrounded by a lot of people and it can be hard for me to get my message to her recorded in the morning, but I am reminded when she sends her recording.

Sometimes we send each other messages throughout the day about what happened or other things we are grateful for. I thank her so often for being consistent. I thank her often for her reflections. She and I are so different as people, yet we see a lot of synchronicities in life and are learning from each other.

This focus on appreciating the little things in life has given us an illusion of being happy and wealthy people.

Let's do the first exercise, I want to get you to start thinking about if you have anyone in your life that you can share your deepest thoughts with. Someone who wants to grow with you. Do you know anyone else who is reading or listening to this book? Would you want to be part of a community of people growing together?

Exercise No. 1:

- Say out loud, who are the first three persons who come to mind that you could share your gratitude with?
- Can you find something right now, in this present moment that you are grateful for?
- Are you brave enough to share it with someone right now? If yes, do that.

This exercise intends to get you to notice the good in your life. To start the journey of shifting focus. When we focus on gratitude we start sending new powerful messages to our subconscious and that in itself is a shit in energy.

We all carry baggage, that affects our illusion. Some of it is leftovers from past lives, but most is baggage from our childhood. Some are, of course, created in our teens or adult life, but they tend to carry less meaning. Most of the heavy burdens are the stuff we tell ourselves as children. It can be baggage that we create ourselves or other people have put upon us. Let's dig into this baggage and what creates it.

♥

Chapter Four

Letting go of guilt, embarrassment, shame and unworthiness

Guilt can be created from remorse, like when we do something that we regret. It can also occur when we feel that we do not live up to social expectations. Embarrassment is often an emotion that occurs when a person feels exposed or vulnerable, often in social situations. In contrast, shame is the inner feeling of inadequacy, not necessarily tied to a specific event. Guilt, embarrassment, and shame can all contribute to a negative self-assessment and are the root of feeling unworthy. These burdens we carry around have nothing to do with our true self. However, this heavy baggage we carry around affects our daily lives, it shapes our reality and our ability to attract wealth.

It is expected to have baggage; however, what sets us apart is how we handle and heal from it. Past baggage shows up in new situations all of the time. When you find yourself triggered and blame others, it's a sign that you have an open wound that needs to be healed. I have noticed that when I start an imaginary conversation in my head with my ex-husband, where I try to defend my actions, I know it is time to look at what is really going on. If I feel guilty before I have taken any action and feel the need to defend my decisions, I know it is something unhealed from my past that is showing up, and if I don't do anything about it, it will drain me from energy.

Are you tired and feel drained by a particular situation? If so, I hope you are ready to heal from what gets in the way of you living a prosperous life. I believe we can indeed have it all.

Guilt, embarrassment, and shame are old emotions stored in the body. They stagnate and clog the positive energy from flowing in your body. If you constantly feel shame, then this is because you believe that you are fundamentally flawed. That your whole self is wrong. These emotions are the core reasons for holding you back and can look and take form in many different ways. Our childhood is filled with these moments. Some emotions were formed because we had a childish mindset, and others because of what others did to us.

Instead of clogging our system, we can use the energy from these memories to create wealth that meets our desires. To transform these memories, we must process them one at a time in the order they come to us.

One of the first memories that I transformed from my childhood is an episode from when I was around seven or eight years old. My mom had given me a ring. The ring was shaped like a snake wrapped around my finger. My mom had brought it home from a trip to Greece. From an adult's perspective, I guess it was a cheap silver ring, but with my childhood eyes, the ring looked very expensive, and I was so happy about it. For three days in a row, I wore it day and night. But on the fourth day, it got caught in my sweater and broke into two pieces. At that moment, I held my breath. My heart stopped. My energy got clogged, and I felt guilty.

I had broken this precious gift. I knew it was an accident but was so embarrassed that I could not tell my mother. I felt like I was not worthy of my mother's love and her gifts. I was sure that she would be mad at me for not being more careful with something so precious. In my head, I made up a story about how I break things and cannot take care of anything of value. "I break things of value" was the story I told myself, and throughout my life, I kept reinforcing this belief. I repeatedly emphasized the emotion of "how I break valuable things".

I don't know how often I have bought a new piece of clothing, and within days, I would have spilled something on it that would make a stain I couldn't get rid of. Even when wealth started to accumulate, the pattern still existed. When I bought my second vintage Louis Vuitton bag, it only took me two months before I ripped the leather on the strap. After that, I purchased a vintage Gucci bag. A couple of months later, I broke the handle. The belief that I break valuable things kept affecting me until I realized that it was a belief I had about myself. I became aware of what I was telling myself. I became aware of what made me think less of myself and what made me ashamed.

As tools to heal from past negative experiences, I like to use either journaling or free writing. Journaling has helped me recognize patterns and self-blaming conversations, whereas freewriting has helped me unlock things I didn't know I had stored in my body.

When I free write, I combine it with unique sound beats called binaural beats. Binaural beats are the sound difference that occurs when you play the same sound in each ear wearing a pair of headphones but at different Hz tones.

To create the beat, you must wear headphones because binaural beats are the sound difference that occurs when you play the same sound in each ear but at different Hz tones. The brain will perceive the difference in Hz as a rhythmic pulsating sound, and this is the binaural beat. It is not a beat that you can play on the radio because it is only possible to create between your ears. The binaural beat influences the brain by altering the states of consciousness, and by doing so, it can improve cognitive functions and enhance different mental states.

There are different types of beats depending on how extensive the range of difference in Hz is. For journaling and meditation, I use Alpha Beats. Those range between 8-13 Hz in difference and give a calm mental state, reducing stress as well as improving focus and concentration. When I first stumbled upon binaural beats, I was amazed that it worked instantly. It is the perfect combination of science and spirituality, and it goes perfectly together with journaling.

Journaling is a method where you write your thoughts and feelings in a book. I like to buy pretty journals that feel good when I touch them. It makes me think that my sacred thoughts are in good hands and are stored safely. I love writing in beautiful journals, but if I don't have one close by when I have thoughts that need to come out, I will use whatever paper I can find to write them down. Sometimes, I will write my thoughts as an email to myself and archive the email later. For those of you who are into journaling, I highly recommend you purchase a workbook that will inspire you. On Amazon, you can find a beautiful workbook for exercises in this book. That option is available to you if you are like me and love that feeling of journaling.

I love journaling and calendars so much that I created a calendar for journaling every day. I will tell you more about how that came to fruition later, but for now, you can know that the Miracle calendar is also another option available both on Amazon worldwide and in all Swedish bookstores.

Freewriting is when you write without stopping so that you don't censor any of your ideas. It doesn't matter if words are misspelled or if the sentences give any meaning. What matters is that you keep writing. You just let the words flow out of you. To free write, you can, for example, set a timer between five and ten minutes and write until the time is done. If you stop writing, the text is lost, and you must start over. This mechanism forces you to keep the words coming out without judging them. There is no time to think, judge, feel, or correct your words. There is only time to let your words flow. This process triggers the brain in new and unexpected ways. I like to use a free online tool found at www.squibler.io/dangerous-writing-prompt-app/. I have no association with them; I simply just like this tool.

Exercise No. 2:

- Choose if you want to journal or free-write.
- Try and remember moments from your childhood when you had bad experiences with something of value or with money.
- Set a timer for 10 minutes.
- Write down memories of when you felt guilt, embarrassment, or shame in the past and reflect on these memories.

Did you do the exercise, or did you think to yourself, 'I will do that later!' Or did you think, 'No, I just want to read or listen to this book and get all the good stuff!'?"

Well, this is where the good stuff begins. So, to progress into a future of complete worthiness, you need to be willing to find some of those moments from your past that are clogging your system.

♥

If you did the first exercise, good for you. I am proud of you. If you didn't, I recommend you do it now. It is 10 minutes of your life. You will feel such satisfaction afterward as the endorphins kick in. You are worthy of that good feeling of accomplishment.

When you have written something, you also want to attach feelings to the story. What were your feelings while doing the first exercise? Can you allow your body to feel those feelings now? For some, it can help to put music on in the background. The music should not contain distractions in the form of words you know, so either listen to instrumental music or music in a language that you do not understand. I encourage you to feel all the emotions that come. Once and for all, decide to forgive yourself. You were a child doing the best that you could.

As I said before, the only thing that is real is the present moment. Everything else is a memory with a perception of what happened in that moment. It is an illusion; the same way guilt and shame are illusions because you have feelings tied to distorted pictures and perceptions of something that has happened in the past. It is your perception of what has happened. Not actual happenings.

We created those feelings in our pasts; therefore, we can also change them. We can charge our memories with new feelings. The brain, our mind, will believe whatever we tell it. So, if your past illusions are not serving you, you can now create new stories and illusions that will serve you better. I like to come up with three different outcomes to past negative experiences. I do this to make sure my brain and the cells in my body recognize that new feelings are connected to the memories. I originally got this exercise from the famous author Pam Grout and have since made it into my own.

Let's take the example of the ring. My first version would be something that seems reasonable to me. I would imagine the ring breaking while it got stuck in my sweater and that I immediately would know that my mom would understand that it was a mistake. I pictured it as a scene from a movie where I would run to her, crying, telling her what happened. She would bend down, dry my eyes, kiss me on my cheeks, and tell me she understood that none of it was my fault. She would give me a huge hug, and I would feel relieved and at peace. I would hear her speak to me just as I speak to my own children. "Stuff like this happens, and material things only have the value we give them". I would feel the warmth of being loved, and my inner child would know that it is okay to make a mistake or accidentally break something.

In the second version, I would go one step further. I would create an intense scenario loaded with powerful emotions. Here, I would break the ring, run to my mom, and she would dry my eyes, kiss my cheeks, and hug me. Then, a woman with balloons would walk by, and my mom would stop her, look at me, and say she recognized my courage and wanted to reward me by buying me a balloon. At this moment, I would feel so proud of myself for immediately telling her the truth. I would realize that material things only have the value we assign them.

In the third version, I would add happiness and some craziness and laugh the whole thing off.

I imagined the whole scenario again, and after my mom would tell me how brave I was, I would feel pride, and the balloon lady would pull out two doves from a birdcage on her wagon that I hadn't noticed until now. I imagined her saying, "As these doves become free, so do the emotions that you have attached to this story; all will be released. As she would release them into the air, she would say, "The doves are free, and so you are you". We would look at the blue sky and laugh as they flew away. This would be a grand, happy moment where I'd feel guilt-free. Breaking the ring would have led me to have these amazing feelings. Thank you, universe, for filling my world with amazing feelings.

In the last version, I would feel free, brave, strong, and encouraged to continue playing. I would realize that sometimes things break, which is merely a sign that I lived my life to the fullest.

Do you see how I slowly built new versions of the event? From one event I could imagine happening to another extraordinary event that would fill my body, my Geist, my lifeforce with new charged happy emotions.

Now it is your turn. Begin by reviewing the words you wrote in exercise two. Look at the memory and try to transform the story.

Exercise No. 3:

- Write your memory again and look at it as a story. Write the new story 2-3 times, and each time, change it in a way that makes it feel happier, stronger, and in your favor. It is okay to let your imagination go wild. It is ok to add people to the story. The purpose is to alter the memory so you can feel better about it in your core. If we are going to carry these altered memories around in our backpacks, it might as well be empowering illusions.

Every time I do this exercise, I consciously carry that emotion with me for the rest of the day. I can feel the strength it has brought to my awareness. I hold my head a little higher, knowing I am present in my life. Also, I know it affects my subconscious for the rest of my life. Some memories and the stories you made up about what happened need more attention than others. My experience is that the lessons I get from them vary from time to time. Therefore, you can do this as often as you want and in all areas of your life.

♥

Using this powerful tool is a way of transforming known circumstances from early childhood into something new. It is a new way of looking at the past. If we look at the present moment of life, there are many influences surrounding us and impacting our lives on a much more subconscious level. What is around you may affect you more than you are aware of.

Let's start with the media and society. Advertisements have been around for hundreds of years. In the mid-19th century, campaigns targeting a specific audience began to appear. For women, for example, a particular soap would make them more refined and elegant and give them a beautiful appearance with brightened skin. On the other hand, for men the soap would make them more masculine.

We have come a long way from media portraying a single black-and-white image of what it means to be the perfect housewife to today's multicolored and multi-size advertisements. Still, advertisement, at its core, is about creating a feeling of not being enough and encouraging you to make purchases that will fill the gap.

The feeling of not being enough is an emotion of lack. There is a perceived gap between what we have and what we believe we need or want. The feeling of lack is rooted in a belief that something essential is missing from our lives. The gap signals that you don't have this or that and that if you had it, you would be fulfilled.

One way the feeling of lack is connected to the feeling of worthiness is through the way we evaluate ourselves and our lives. We may question our worth when we feel like we lack something, whether it's material possessions, social connections, or personal qualities.

In our society, there is a strong connection between the accumulation of wealth and possessions as a measure of success and social status. I am all for buying whatever makes you happy. Still, if you want the stuff and the social status to numb the feeling of lack, then the emotionally charged energy is not being handled. You will feel equally or even more empty on the inside even if you surround yourself with more stuff. This is why we need to address the root cause of your feeling of lack and unworthiness.

Our true sense of value comes from within. The unique qualities that make us who we are and how we use those qualities are what contribute to a meaningful world. Therefore, it is so important that you focus on cultivating self-acceptance, compassion for self, and gratitude for what you do have. Doing so can shift our perspective away from lack towards a more profound sense of worthiness and fulfillment, which is precisely what I have done.

I have made the most changes in my life around healing my past relationship with money and things of value, self-acceptance, self-compassion, and daily gratitude for what I already have. I truly believe that is why I went from almost bankrupt to becoming a millionaire. I worked and continue working on these areas and will share my practices with you throughout the book.

Something that ignites a spark in me is reading about other successful women: I feel that if it is possible for her, it is possible for me, and I can do whatever I set my mind to.

When I can create that emotion in my body and soul, I transform my belief about what is possible for me. This is when I start to attract situations that will take me closer to my goal. I hope that is the feeling this book is creating in you. Sometimes my judgment of myself gets in the way of my success. Negative beliefs will prevent the flow of attracting the good stuff therefore, I have a good habit of noticing it and clearing it out.

I am embarrassed to say it, but I judge much more than I want to admit. It happens all the time. Just last week, I was flying home from Italy, and at the tax-free shop, there was a woman in front of me in the line. On her head, holding her hair back, were the best-looking Gucci sunglasses I had ever seen. She had the Louis Vuitton carry-on. She had an expensive watch and a perfect manicure. Everything about her was perfect.

My thoughts were going on, and on, about how she could not have bought that lifestyle herself. I looked at her husband to see if the money came from his or her family. I caught myself judging here. I could feel my flow starting to spiral down and stopped immediately. I decided to send her love and make up a new story. I projected my new higher self on her. If I could create that lifestyle for myself, why wouldn't it be possible for her to create the same? Even if all the material stuff had been gifted to her, that would mean that she was exceptionally good at attracting money and cool gifts into her life. I should become the student and let her be my teacher. I looked at her with new eyes. Eyes of humbleness and thankfulness.

When we stop ourselves from destructive thoughts about others, something amazing happens in the body. New signals are built in the brain, telling the monkey brain that you are in charge. You might still judge (a lot), but when you become aware of it, you stop your thoughts from repeating themselves every day, and that is the start of new thoughts, habits, and actions.

Now let's look at when your judgments get in the way of your success. I want you to take out your journal or freewriting tool and prepare for the next exercise.

Exercise No. 4:

- Set the timer for ten minutes.
- Write down three times when you judged someone else recently.
- Write what you were saying about them.
- Reflect upon whether what you said about them in any way, form, or shape, reflects how you feel about yourself.

This exercise is important because it often reveals what you think of your own worthiness. What you say about others is what you subconsciously are saying about yourself or revealing a fear you have about yourself.

♥

I hope I can congratulate you on a good job writing down your judgmental thoughts. Can I? Were there any judgments that relate to yourself? Did you identify any fears that you put upon yourself? Can you relate your judgments or fears to repeated patterns of behavior?

Seeing these connections to the past, I believe you can choose to use them in two ways. Nondestructive or destructive, you repeatedly talk about who did what and how that affected you as if you were not in charge or had no responsibility in the situation. When you repeat stories like that, you are repeating your past. It is usual for the brain to repeat familiar old stories and patterns for several reasons.

To begin with, the brain is designed to conserve energy and resources. It constantly monitors the body's internal state, ensuring we have enough energy to perform essential functions. By repeating known patterns, the brain can rely on existing neural pathways and avoid spending extra energy one creating new ones. It is energy-saving to repeat what you have done before.

Another reason we repeat the experience, even if it is a bad experience, is that there is comfort and familiarity in it. Especially if you live in a stressful or uncertain environment, your brain wants to repeat familiar patterns to reduce your stress level and maintain a sense of control. It is comfortable. It is simple, and it works.

Lastly, the brain's primary responsibility is to regulate bodily functions and behaviors. Most importantly, it keeps us alive. It is safer to repeat what you have done in the past because your past behaviors have proven to keep you alive.

However, I want to be more than just alive, and I guess so do you. I want to live life to its fullest. Therefore, I choose to use these connections to our past in a more constructive and healing way.

My goal is to heal from old baggage and trauma I carry whenever they show up. I look at past fears and old judgments and either change the energy around the story, as in the story about the ring I broke, or I notice that I have a pattern and actively choose to do something different. By stepping outside our comfort zones and trying new things, we can challenge our brains to form new neural pathways, which is how we grow. This is how we create a new future different from our past.

Cleaning up the energy from past experiences is necessary to elevate your energy. It might not be nice when you are doing it, but it is nice when you are on the other side. Sometimes, it is done in minutes; other times it takes longer, but it is all possible with practice and time.

I believe the easiest way of changing patterns is by setting my intention and affirming the person I want to be as if I already were that person. Simply put, setting an intention is when you guide your thoughts, behaviors, and actions toward a specific goal or outcome. Affirmations are statements that reinforce positive beliefs about yourself or a particular situation. They are declarations that something is true in the present. This has been the easiest method for me, and it has had the most significant impact on moving my mindset from broke to millionaire.

I love intention setting so much that I have devoted a whole chapter to it. But first, let's dig deep into the science behind why intentions and affirmations work.

♥

Chapter Five

What is epigenetics and how it can help you

The year before we started the health and wellness center, I looked into different programming classes and schools. However, I couldn't see myself scaling down my life. I wasn't ready to give up my high-income life with vacations in Greece, two cars, and a boat. The life I was living, with the beliefs I had, I couldn't imagine how going back to school would be possible. There was no one else in my life who could see that either. So, I didn't do more with the thought other than plant a seed.

After being almost bankrupt, my only asset was the roof over my head; I knew I needed a safe place to land to lick my wounds and rebuild my energy. I got a job as a receptionist at a spa hotel.

The reception was a perfect place because my job was just to be kind to people, smile all day, and welcome them to our town. To genially meet people, look them in the eyes, and say "Hi, welcome to this amazing spa". It was good for my soul. Most of the guests were happy to be there. Some had saved for years to come to our little town, others came for work, but most of them were couples celebrating love. All day, I was surrounded by love. People were kissing, hugging, and looking deep into each other's eyes.

Seeing all that love helped me rebuild my belief in people and filled my cells with new energy. Getting free access to the spa at certain times of the day was, of course, another nice step in the healing process.

While I was at the spa, I remembered that seed I had planted a couple of years earlier about returning to school. Suddenly, it sounded like a good idea; because of student loans and government funding, this would be another safe place to continue healing and an opportunity for self-growth. I applied for a student loan and to a bachelor's program in informatics. Both applications were accepted.

Becoming a student would provide a financially stable period in my life. I would have precisely the amount I thought I needed to pay all my bills, be able to put food on the table, and even have money to indulge in small adventures with the kids.

Not long after I had begun studying, I stumbled upon the subject of epigenetics, which finally gave me a scientific way of explaining all the "hippie stuff" I was doing. It also confirmed my gut feeling that I was on the right path. It made sense that I could finally combine my rational and scientific side with the more soft and emotional side, where spiritual healing, belief in the law of attraction, affirmations, and intention setting played a huge part in my life.

I learned from biologist Docktor Bruce H. Lipton, that studies in epigenetics started in 1949 but that it didn't take off until 1987 at Stanford University. Today, there are ongoing studies in all major universities. In fact, there are more than half a million published research articles in Google Scholar about epigenetics. So, what is epigenetics?

Let me break it down for you. To start, the science of epigenetics shows us how our genes are reprogrammed to do something different than what our DNA tells our genes to do. The cell membrane gets information from its surrounding environment and uses this information to control gene activity. This means that it is not our DNA that determines how our lives turn out, but instead, it is the information we put in our cell membrane that determines the outcome. Scientists have tested removing genes (DNA) from the cells and discovered that the cells could survive and become whatever the body needed.

Epigenetics research shows that we can alter our gene expression without altering our DNA by reducing stress, changing to a healthier diet, and removing toxins and drugs from our system. Not only that, our thoughts, emotions, and behavior also have a massive impact on our cell membrane.

Let me give you an example. If you are overweight and have type 2 diabetes just like one of your biological parents, it is not because of the genes from your parent; It is because you eat the same types of foods, wear the same types of clothes, sit and watch TV for the same number of hours and are surrounded by the same types of people as your parent. Your physical and mental world is similar to that of your parents, and when you have the same environment as them, you create the same type of environment in your cell membrane, sending the same type of signals between cells, which produce the same types of diseases in the body.

If you want a different life or future than your parents, you need to create it. This might be scary, but it can also be inspiring because that means you are in charge. You can control your environment. You can learn to control your thoughts, attitude, and behavior. When you finally control this, you are vibrationally ready to create your future and let money flow to you. Let me give you an example.

You have probably heard about the placebo effect. It is an excellent example of how our thoughts affect our cells and what happens in our physical bodies. The first experiment with a placebo effect was documented back in 1799. Science repeatedly shows that if a person gets a sugar pill instead of the actual medicine and believes that it is the real medicine, they will show a significant improvement in their health or be cured entirely. It is proven that the happy, trustful energy we fill our bodies with will create the change we need on a cellular level. Science has proven that when we think that something positive will happen, it will happen.

Did you know that science has also proven the opposite? About 150 years ago, scientists started researching something called nocebo. For example, if a person reads the table of contents about possible negative side effects of a medicine, some of them will believe that they are amongst those who will get a negative side effect. Science shows that even if these people get a sugar pill instead of real medicine, they are still able to create negative effects and cause a decrease in their health. For example, in one study, people used their minds to visualize the worst effects. The visualizations were so powerful that they manifested in their bodies just as they were expected and gave them the imagined side effects or decreased their health.

Still, there is no reason to walk around in fear of anything. It is not like we will think one unhealthy thought about ourselves, and it will happen. We truly must believe it in our core down to a cellular level. The same mechanisms that are at play when we talk about how placebo and nocebo affect our health can be used to attract wealth and abundance.

One definition of manifestation is the process of bringing something into existence using intention and belief. It involves visualizing and feeling what we desire as if it has already happened and trusting that the universe will bring it to us.

I love how Dr. Joe Dispenza, so well, explains how the connection between feeling our future on a cellular level and changing our thoughts will shape our beliefs and reality. When we tap into a deep sense of knowing that our desired future is already ours, we begin to align our thoughts and actions with that reality and attract the future that we want.

Changing our thoughts and beliefs is an ongoing process that requires consistent effort and repetition since we are influenced by our past experiences and the beliefs of those around us. Inherited patterns from our pasts and our parents can be deeply ingrained in us. That is why it takes intentional effort to shift our mindset and adopt new beliefs that support our desired future. To succeed, we must make future emotions more important than emotions from our past.

By actively working on shifting our thoughts and beliefs on a cellular level, in the present moment, towards beliefs that support our desired future, we can create the reality we want.

Just like a placebo effect, where the belief of healing produces real improvements in health, our beliefs and thoughts about money and wealth have the power to improve our financial situation and shape our new reality. Sometimes, we need to look at our past to move forward.

I believe that humanity evolved for each generation because we are here to explore and learn and also because our parents wanted a better life for us than they had themselves. Yet, we tend to repeat many of our parents' patterns. My mother moved to a school for sewing and design when she was young, and I moved to the US at fifteen to go to high school. Similarly, we both moved out of our parent's house at a young age.

I believe that we both grew tremendously because we moved out of our parents' houses at a young age. I want my children to move out at a young age. Not as young as me and their grandmother, but still young because I believe it will shape them and help them grow. This way, my family will repeat a positive pattern in our legacy.

As a collective species, we can have different experiences and still have the same outcome. My family believes that moving away from home at a young age is positive. In Italy, for example, they have the opposite beliefs and don't move out from their parents' house until they are in their thirties. Italians are equally successful, and there is no judgment on my part. It just goes to show that whatever you believe to be right will become right for you. It can be the opposite of another person's beliefs and still work out great for both of you.

The thoughts we have about our ancestors will affect our future. You can choose to blame those who have gone before you, or you can choose to have positive thoughts and use them to empower you. I know I have done both. Let me tell you about an example from my family.

Besides being an outstanding entrepreneur, creating value in new and unexplored areas, my grandfather was also an alcoholic. Sometimes, he would disappear for days at a time. I remember my grandmother told me about this incident back in the late fifties. She had put aside money in the company's savings account because she intended to pay a bill to a building material company of almost one million Danish crowns. It was a lot of money at that time and still is today. I can't even believe the building material company would extend them such a huge credit. But I guess that was the way it was when you had big building projects. Anyway, the day came when my grandmother had the money in the bank, and she wrote the building material company a cheque for a million Danish crowns and sent it in the mail.

The building material company called her a few days later and told her the cheque had bounced. She couldn't understand what had happened. Then, my grandfather came home from one of his trips and told her he had bought a hotel to help a friend in financial trouble.

He had been drunk, impulsive, and just wanted to help a friend. I may have romanticized the stories of his disappearances and his kindness my whole childhood, but make no mistake, his alcoholism destroyed his marriage and eventually killed him. Unfortunately, at least two of his four children would repeat the same pattern and become alcoholics. One even ended up in a two-month coma and nearly died before turning his life around. The other one was my mom.

As we all know, alcoholism is a disease. We can dispute whether this disease is present in my body because of DNA or if it is an inherited behavioral pattern. It really doesn't matter to me since I know that either way, it can be treated with the help of epigenetics. I know that by actively making different choices in my life, such as changing my eating and drinking behavior, as well as changing the way I think and consciously choosing who I surround myself with, I will receive different results in my life compared to what my family's history otherwise would dictate. Instead of carrying guilt and shame about my family's history, this knowledge has empowered me, and I share it with you because I have this burning desire to empower you to do the same.

We are not destined to inherit or replicate our parent's negative patterns. Once we become aware of these patterns, we have the power to heal and transform them into something positive and turn a new leaf. Therefore, we will use exercise number five to increase our awareness. This is a crucial step towards creating positive change and building momentum in our journey towards healing.

Start by taking out your journal or freewriting tool and set a timer for 10 minutes. Turn off all social media such as Facebook, Instagram, Twitter, or whatever you have on all your electronic devices, particularly your phone. If you are home and other people are in the house, ensure that you are in a different room. This is only ten minutes. Ten minutes for you because you matter. You and your future matter today. You are worthy of your time, and what is important to you matters. Find your perfect space and set the timer.

Exercise No. 5:

I want you to free write for ten minutes and reflect on the questions below:

- What negative patterns of your parents or family have you repeated that have affected how you look at money and wealth?
- Which negative patterns concerning your finances have you actively broken and made different choices than what your family otherwise would have done?

Our thoughts about money affect many areas of our lives. We won't see any growth if we don't think we are worthy. So Sweety, please, let me reassure you that you are worthy! You are worthy of the good life, the luxury, the security, and all of the possibilities that money brings.

♥

I changed my shopping behavior once I realized I was worthy of this. Not only did I shop in different stores, but I also shopped differently. One of my patterns was buying clothes from a cheap online store. I searched for the most affordable items and looked for discounts. After a wash or two, my clothes would often get loose fitting or out of shape. My closet was filled with unworn clothes that were either too small or too big. I had bought them because they were a bargain, thinking that if they didn't fit me, perhaps my daughter could use them someday. Moreover, my bed sheets were the cheapest kind. I used to believe that the quality of bed sheets didn't matter since I only slept on them.

I was unaware of how my perception of myself affected other areas of my life. When I started setting clear intentions and healing my past, I shifted how I saw myself and my self-worth. This change also had a positive influence on how I shopped. I started to focus on quality over quantity and on acting as my future self in this present moment. Maybe you have heard of the expression " dress for the job you want"? My expression is, "Dress for the life you want to live"!

I believe that conscious purchasing is an act of self-love. With the intention of reinforcing my sense of worth and boosting my self-confidence, I set up three shopping rules for myself:

- · I am worthy of quality.
- · I dress for the life I want to live.
- · The clothes should fit well and feel fabulous.

What started as a simple rule turned into affirmations. These positive statements I repeated when shopping did something good for my personal growth.

The affirmation "I am worthy of quality" not only turned out to be about my clothes but also transpired into other areas. For example, on my student budget, I went to the cheapest bed linen store and bought the highest quality bed sheets. I was getting myself the best quality I believed I could afford and went straight home and changed my bed sheets.

Going to bed every night, I would tell myself I was worthy of quality in my life. I said it until it was imprinted in the cellular membrane surrounding my DNA. This was one way I used epigenetics to change the signals in my body. I know now that I am worthy of quality, and the things I do not need or want anymore might do good for others. I gave all of my old bed sheets to my friend, a skipper who could use them to clean the engine on her boat. It felt good to give away what no longer served a purpose in my life as it created space and freedom. It also felt good to know that the items would be reused and serve a new purpose for someone else.

"Dress for the life you want to live" is still an on-going process. My closet wasn't changed overnight, but I found that cleaning it out from old clothes made space for new ones. Not because I wanted to consume more but because I wanted the clothes, I was wearing to bring me joy and tell my body, mind, and cell membrane that I am the person I want to become. That is why I look through my closet about every three months and ask myself: "Is this what the broke Mette would wear, or is it what the millionaire Mette would wear"? Asking the right questions guides me forward in both the cleansing process and in using epigenetics to change my future into abundance and luxury.

The affirmation that: "The clothes should fit and feel fabulous" was later changed to "I wear clothes that fit and feel fabulous"! It sounds almost the same, but there is a difference in the energy the affirmation gives. The latter affirmation gave me more self-confidence and was empowering. I often repeated the affirmation and felt what I was saying was the truth, which created new neural pathways in my brain that supported a real change and made it my new belief.

To facilitate the feeling, I put up a note inside my closet asking myself if I was dressing for the broke Mette or the rich Mette. It was a choice I had to make daily, and yes, sometimes I dressed for the Mette with the attitude of: "I don't care, I am just quickly running to the store"! We all have free choice, and it is an ongoing process.

Although it might sound like the most straightforward idea, it took me until I reached forty before I stopped buying clothes that were too small. I had a false belief I would eventually fit in them after losing weight. The importance of believing that we are worthy of being loved the way we are right now, in this moment, cannot be stressed enough. When I tell myself that the clothes should fit and feel fabulous, I also tell myself that I am worthy of being loved. I am worthy of self-love. When I am worthy of self-love, I can create the life I want and feel good about money. It is all connected.

By transforming how we look at our outer world, just like we can transform our closets, we can transform how we look upon ourselves and set a foundation for financial growth. The following exercise is for you to examine your closet to see how many pieces of clothes there are in there that genuinely represent the person you want to be compared to how many pieces of clothing there are that no longer represent you.

Exercise No. 6:

 · Make two or three affirmations that fit your future you.

· Look at your clothes and identify those that no longer represent you.
· Clean your closet and give away the clothes you no longer need.

This exercise can be done all over the house. Do you deserve to have lifeless, dry tubes lying around your bathroom, with old, stagnated energy, or are you worthy of surrounding yourself with things that bring you happiness? Look around in your kitchen and inspect your cabinets. Do you have containers with no lids or lids that don't fit the containers? Are you so poor that you need to clog your cabinets with lids and unmatching containers, or can you declutter your cabinets and raise your standard by keeping your house in order so that it matches the new you? Decluttering can be fun, but it can also be irritating. If we go back to how our brains work, this exercise will challenge it. It can be uncomfortable because it challenges the beliefs we have about ourselves. It requires energy, but I promise that the new space created by decluttering will also give you fresh energy and help make room for new, exciting things to happen in your life. Also, it will remind the brain of the new person you are creating. Let the process take as long as it needs. As I mentioned before, this is an ongoing process. We are transforming the core of who we really are. Some changes come directly, and others take practice.

♥

By cleaning in the real world outside our brain and body, the inside of our body is transformed. This happens because new neural pathways are made in our brains. By using epigenetics, we change the signals to our cell membranes. We no longer let our DNA run the show. We run the show. By now, I hope you know your worth. You are important and worthy of the best.

Epigenetics shows us that what we tell ourselves in one aspect of life, will affect all aspects of our lives. On a material level, we can facilitate change in our gene expression by cleaning out the closets and cabinets. In contrast, on a physical and spiritual level, it happens when we change how we consume foods, exercise, or meditate. Meditation has long been known to reduce stress, improve immune function, and reduce inflammation, but did you know that we also can use it to manifest affirmations?

Mostly, I use guided meditations, or storytelling, to lift my energy and align my thoughts, emotions, and beliefs.

The following exercise I often do before falling asleep. I first heard about it from the famous author Pam Grout, and then, over the years, I have made it into my own by incorporating different teachings into it. I often do it at night to carry the feeling with me into sleep. But if I do it in the morning, I try to stay in the feeling for five to ten minutes in meditation before starting the day.

I use storytelling to lift my energy to a new level, which is what this next exercise is about. The way we will use storytelling this time is to make a story about you. You are the main character and the most important person. Actually, there doesn't need to be other people in your story if you don't want to. You decide. Think of it as a commercial for the perfect life of the rich you. There are only a few scenes, or maybe there is just one screen. I will guide you through all the sound effects and emotional appeal.

It is fine to wait and do this exercise until right before you go to sleep tonight. Just because repeating new habits is a good way of making them stick, you should consider doing it twice, once now and then for a second time when you go to bed.

Exercise No. 7:

You are making a movie about yourself in the future as a rich person. You will play out the same scene three times, but you will change it slightly every time.

When you do it in the evening, play the movie as many times as you want to and stay in the good, wealthy feeling until you fall asleep.

  · Sit or lay in a comfortable position with your eyes
    closed.

First movie:

- Imagine yourself in the future at a place where you want to be.
- Look at yourself in the third person, meaning look at yourself from the outside.
- Imagine yourself wealthy. What does wealth, financial freedom, and abundance look like to you?
- Turn on your senses.
- Are you inside in a house or outside in a garden or nature?
- Listen to the sounds surrounding you. Is there music playing in the background? If so, what song is playing?
- What does it smell like where you are?
- What clothes are you wearing? How does it feel against your skin?
- Are you eating? If so, what does it taste like?
- What are you doing?
- How do you feel?

Now, imagine you are taking out your phone and logging into your bank accounts.

- What amount do you see in your savings account?
- What amount do you see in your spending account?

Now, log into your stock account.

· What are your stocks worth?

Pay attention to how you feel in this moment. Can you appreciate how far you have come?

Before you move to the next scene, I want you to adjust the situation slightly. Perhaps now you have a business and want to check your business account? Or maybe you want to check your email and see that you just received a pay raise? Try to find as many areas as possible in life where you want to see financial growth and make a way of visualizing it.

The second time you play the movie, you are in this fantastic place and feel grateful for all the financial growth you have received. In this grateful state, you start checking your balances and feel utter joy.

- Add other areas where you wish to see growth and expansion.
- Have you received any gifts lately? How do they look? Are you wearing any of those gifts?
- Do you drive a new car?
- Do you have a picture of your house in your wallet?
- Go wild and crazy. Feel the luxury of your new life in every cell of your body and play the movie again.
- You are living your dream in this movie. Can you feel it?

Look how far you have come. Stay in this moment for a while. Acknowledge your growth. Breathe, feel it, and congratulate yourself. You are amazing.

I now want to challenge you for the third time, playing the movie. It contains all the good stuff from the second time, but this time, you play the movie in first person, meaning you experience everything as if it were through your own eyes. This takes a little practice, so just be happy with whatever result you get and notice how you get better and better each time.

- Play the movie.
- Feel it all the way deep into your cells.
- Stay in the feeling for five to ten minutes.

This exercise can be done as often as you want. For some time, you might want to do it daily. This exercise is done to let your body and neural pathways know that this is the new you and to let your desired future be more important than your past experiences.

Now that you are in a new state of feeling, I intend to show diversity in ways of becoming financially wealthy and healing the conversations we have with ourselves about what is possible. Let me take you even further and get that gut feeling turned on all the way.

♥

Chapter Six

Trust your gut feeling and fill up your spirit

Remember that nothing is wrong with you! Everything is right with you. Source doesn't make mistakes. I call it Source or Universe. Perhaps you refer to it as God, Allah, Great Spirit, or Elohim. It doesn't matter to me who or what you believe in; there are no rights or wrongs. All there is to life are our life journeys, experiences, learnings, and evolvements. That is all there is to life. The rest are interpretations and memories and those we can change.

You have done your best based on the information you had. You only live this particular life once, so be gentle with yourself. Just by reading or listening to this book, you are actively taking steps toward becoming a new you. So, lift your head and give yourself a pat on the back. Stand tall and be proud that you dare to make new choices. I am so proud of you and thank you from the bottom of my heart that you want to take this journey with me. It is a journey we share. Today, you are reading my book; tomorrow, I might be reading your book. We exchange energy and are in this together.

In this context, recognizing your worth and being kind to yourself is essential to self-improvement. When we judge and diminish ourselves, we tell our bodies and minds that we are incapable. We slowly kill our spirits and our gut feelings. What we need to do is the total opposite. We need to have compassion for ourselves and ignite that fire inside us. Once we master that, we can trust our gut feelings and act accordingly.

Before we focus on the fire inside us, the gut feeling, and the filling up spirit, I want to make you relaxed and get back to the theme of old dreams.

Exercise No. 8:

- Slow down and take a deep breath. Inhale for 1, 2, 3, 4. Feel the energy moving from the bottom of your stomach in a spiral movement all the way up to your head and even above your head. Exhale for 1, 2, 3, 4. Repeat, inhale for 1, 2, 3, 4, and move the energy from your pelvis through your stomach, up in your chest, through your throat, and face, and move it up just above your head, and exhale for 1, 2, 3, 4. Do it one last time.

Now, when you have slowed down, feeling more relaxed, and have your breathing under control, it is time to explore old dreams or seeds you planted in your life earlier.

- Time to take out your journal.
- Position yourself comfortably.
- Turn off the volume on your phone, including notifications for all your social media apps.
- Set a timer for ten minutes and turn on some instrumental music.

You should be alone in the room so no one can interrupt you. This is important because you need to allow your mind to wander into a heightened state of awareness.

It is time to free-write. Let the words pour into your journal. It doesn't matter if the sentences make sense or if you make spelling errors. The important thing is to keep writing continually and undisturbed for ten minutes.

Write down your answers to the following questions:

- What dreams did you have when you were younger?
- What seeds have you planted in your mind earlier but didn't water enough at the time for them to bloom?

The reason for this exercise is to remember what has inspired you in the past. It took me two years from when I first looked into programming classes until I started my bachelor's degree in programming. It took two years because I feared how it would affect me financially. I doubted I could provide for my children and didn't know how it would affect their lives and mine.

When I began my programming studies, I noticed how my fear of not having enough money also manifested in the people around me. For instance, many of my close family members, except my sister, showed concern about my decision to quit my job and start studying. Fortunately, my sister trusted my decision and supported and encouraged me, which meant a lot. It can be hard to follow a gut feeling if those around you are critiquing your decision, but still, it is important that you trust that feeling inside of you.

Making life-changing decisions takes a lot of courage. Your soul needs to remember your dreams, and your mind needs to long for them and nourish them to come to fruition. You see, there will come a time when you know in your heart what direction you need to take. It will not be possible to ignore it because ignoring it will hurt you to your core, both physically and mentally.

It helped me look into different options so that my final decision would be well thought through. I could feel in my stomach what options weren't the best fit for me and what areas I needed to explore further. Simply put, you need to start where you are now and then be willing to continue to explore your options and imagine where you want to be and how you want to feel.

Do you need to make a life-changing decision? Consider if you are where you want to be in life. Are you financially free, live a luxurious life, wealthy, and feel abundance? If not, I believe you are ready to let your dreams blossom and become the best version of yourself!

For me, I started slowly to trust my gut feeling again. I knew that I had to continue to share my knowledge. I have always loved being on stage. I like the energy. I feel confident on stage, and I know that I make a difference.

I had this newfound knowledge of epigenetics that gave me the connection between science and the fluffy stuff of healing. I call it the fluffy stuff because a lot of people I meet in politics, doctors, and other people in high positions would share, in confidence, that they would have visions and gut feelings, but they couldn't put words on it.

In the professions, they were in, it was not allowed to talk about it in any other way than from a scientifically proven way, so for them, it was like being dragged back and forth. The gut feeling would be this deep sense of knowing what the answer is in opposition to scientific, evidence-based knowledge, where you gather as much information as you can to support your thesis. Epigenetics was the bridge between the two.

I felt a need to share the evidence-based science behind Epigenetics and manifestation, but I didn't know how. And then the universe does what the universe always does when you have set an intention, it puts the right people in front of you (or me in this case).

I was walking down the stairs of city hall and bumped into a person from the Study Association. She told me some of her latest insights and I told her mine. She got excited and encouraged me to organize a public lecture. She was willing to help with a small part of the funding.

This meeting gave me the spark I needed, and within a few weeks, I had put together a team consisting of the event coordinator, sound, lights, and cameras. I knew I wanted to record it so that I could use it later for course content. Not that I had online courses at the time, but that was another seed in my garden of dreams, waiting to happen in the future.

Together with the local bookstore, I started to sell tickets, and then Covid hit. Everything was shot down. We were no longer allowed to be 100 people in the room; we were allowed to be eight people. I doubted how I would finance the venue and pay the crew if I couldn't sell tickets.

I did what I always do when I find myself in an energy of fear: I go back to the intention and use the tools I give you in this book. I free write about what I want to accomplish, I meditate, and I listen to my gut.

Solutions are often found in the areas where you least expect them, and that is why it is important to listen to your gut. It turned out that another project where I was volunteering had received a lot of money for a charity event, but because of Covid, we couldn't use the money as intended. I did an inspired action and asked if we could use the money to host my event if I would turn it into a fundraiser for the same cause. My wish was granted, I now had the money.

So my talk ended up being a Facebook live charity event where we raised funds for girls in India who risked being sold to marry older men. It felt so good. It was good for the girls. It was good for the crew; they all got paid eventually, and It was good for me because now I had physical proof that I could listen to my gut and manifest into fruition again.

I knew that I wanted to do more talks, and I also knew it had to wait a little bit. Just like the last time I made something big happen, the actual growing part took energy. There were a lot of lessons for me to learn, and I had to land on my new knowledge.

Changing your mindset and exploring new paths can be scary, but the universe will confirm that you are on the right path by putting the right people in your path. Your job is to listen with an open heart and to trust your gut just like I did with the women on the stairs of city hall.

The universe will confirm the good choices by sending good energy. It can come in many ways, sometimes it is via songs, dance or simply feeling good. One example was the feeling I had on stage; another was the feeling I had on the first day of school.

Our class of about 300 students was divided into smaller groups for us to get to know each other better. I was in a group with a 22-year-old e-sporter who had competed in the US. He told me his background and concerns. He said he didn't know if he had time to go to school because he was making good money from his sport, so he wasn't sure what to prioritize. He looked at me and said that he felt really old when he came to school that morning and saw all the 19-year-olds. That was until he met me.

I found it funny that a 22-year-old young man would feel old in a school full of people who were two to three years younger than him. Being 42 years old, I was the oldest person in the class. I was proud of it. I was filled with many happy feelings on that first day of school. I knew that I was in the right place.

Returning to school in my forties gave me another way of looking at school. I approached it as if it were a job and was there every day from 8 a.m. to 4 p.m. Having life experience is a great advantage when studying because the brain has already established existing memories to which you can attach new knowledge, making it easier to remember and apply new information. If education is on your list of dreams, then I highly recommend it. If it is not your dream, that is fine too. It is not for everyone. Your dream might look totally different. There is no right and wrong here, only your true path.

Our dreams are one thing, our values another. For me, it became evident that I wanted to show my children what chances you can have in life by getting yourself an education. It is no secret that one of my children sees no point in going to school. Honestly, I am pretty sure I didn't see any point with school when I was his age, either. Actually, I was kicked out of a private school in 5th grade because I behaved unacceptably to the teacher. I will tell you that story another time. The important thing here is that I know that my growth over the last few years has sparked ideas in him. That is good enough for me.

It is important to me to teach my children that if you go to school, you can change your whole life. For me, that is an important lesson. For you, it might be something else. In other words, when you look at your values, they can also give you a clue to what is important to you and inspire you to take new actions.

Values and dreams make up a powerful fuel inside of you. When you are in contact with those, you can make anything happen. It is one of those cliches that are true.

The previous exercise was for you to remember what was important to you as a child. I hope it triggered and opened a connection to your body and that you remember what made you happy as a child. Remember to water the seeds of your dreams. Now, it is time to let your dreams grow at their own pace and focus on your gut feelings.

Trusting your gut feelings is all about getting you excited about life. It is about getting to a place where you can feel your future. We can use childhood dreams and values to get ourselves started. We can also use intentions and affirmations to create the future we want.

Many of us are raised believing that we are deficient somehow. This creates a perceived gap between our desires and our current state. We are taught that there is a gap between what we want and where we are today. That gap is in our minds and our thoughts. When we do exercises like the ones we did earlier, where we feel our future in the present, the gap is eliminated because we tell our mind and body that we are already there. The amazing thing is that the mind believes what you tell it. One study showed that when people imagined that they worked out for a certain amount of time, the result in the body was as much as half of those who did it in real life, which is far more than nothing.

I am amazed and intrigued by how we can use the brain to our advantage. We can ignite our trust in our gut feelings by journaling on old dreams, meditating on our futures, and self-reflecting on questions like "What are my values?" In a later chapter, we will use creative expression through vision boarding as a way of igniting our spirits.

Knowing your "what" and "why" is another way to understand your behavior. When I interviewed the Instagram profile Miljonarmamman for the chapter about investments, she told me that her first goal was to have stocks worth a million Swedish kronor. Being unemployed, she set this goal for herself right after her maternity leave. Seven years later, that dream had come true. I will give you all of her financial advice and Money tips later, but for now, let's stay focused on why she was able to do it. She was clear on her goal. She wanted to change her financial situation. She didn't work harder, but she worked dedicated, knowing her "what" and "why."

A hike in the woods, sitting by a lake or the ocean, or a simple walk in a park are ways of helping you feel more grounded and in tune with your natural rhythms. It will connect you to your true self and fill up your spirit.

If possible, I suggest you do this next exercise barefooted in nature. It can be on grass or in the forest. If it's winter when you read this, maybe you could go for an ice bath and sauna. I challenge you to find a way to get into nature.

Exercise No. 9:

- Find a place in nature.
- Think about 3-4 things:
    - **What** do you want to change in your life?
    - **Why** do you want to change those things?

Your time is now. Take the time you need for this exercise. If you don't have your journal close by when you are done with the exercise, you could write a note to yourself on your phone or send an email to yourself. It is an easy way to keep a record of it. Because you wrote it down, it will also have a better imprint in your body's cells, making it real to you.

♥

Chapter Seven

Understand where you want to go

Now that you worked on trusting your gut feeling and understood your "What" and "Why," let's increase the fire. We want that flame to burn so fiercely that it will persist through rainy weather and storms. The fire inside you will help navigate and guide you through those darker days. Transformation might be painful sometimes but have faith that it is good on the other side.

Let's continue to shed the beliefs of the past. You are unstoppable. You are a fierce person, an intelligent person. Are you ready to change your belief system? You are unstoppable. In my heart, I genuinely believe that the world is open to you and you can accomplish anything you set your mind to.

Finding what fuels you is individual, but throughout the book, I am returning to the feeling of feeling rich because that is a dam good fuel and motivator.

I will give you an example of what made me feel rich. In 2020, I was on a ferry on my way out to Koster Island. A lady I recognized came onboard with two large Louis Vuitton bags; to me, that was the ultimate sign of luxury and wealth.

I felt in my body that this would be me within a short amount of time. I truly felt that that could be me. As broke as I was that day on the ferry, I still believe that it could be me. Two years later, it was me. One of my bags is so big that my friend suggested I could sleep in it. Now, buying an endless number of bags has no meaning to me, but these two symbolized my personal growth. It was a testimony to who I had become. I wonder if you have something in mind that will symbolize your personal growth.

In the next exercise, we will dig into what fuels you. Have you ever looked at something and felt that this could also be yours one day? Or wonder what people do for a living to be able to afford that house or that car? Well, It can be yours, and you deserve whatever you dream of.

You will make a vision board in this exercise, but we are renaming it. It is not only a vision board; it is an action board because it will require you to take action when opportunities occur. I credit Dr. Tara Swart Bieber for teaching me that brain research shows that action boards effectively attract what you want. I had done them before, but with this research, it is scientifically documented.

In plain, simple words, you could say that all your brain wants from you is that you should survive long enough to reproduce. So it is trying really hard to protect you from danger. It will take the shortest, easiest, and safest road to get you from A to B.

To protect you from drama, uncomfortable situations, or danger, the brain suggests something else you could do, like overwork, eating, drinking, drugs, or just zooming out by lying on the couch watching TV. It is an easy and safe way to spend the day.

Your brain considers anything new a threat to your survival and tries to find as many excuses as possible for you not to go down that road. I will come back later in the book about how to overcome your excuses and give you directions on how to make your action board, but for now, let's focus on why action boards work.

When your mind sees the images daily, it makes different associations and thoughts about them. On a daily basis, you will have some thought related to your dream, so when an actual real-life opportunity turns up that can take you closer to your dream, your brain will say, "Hay, I have seen this path before, that is a safe one, we can go down that road" and that will make it easier for you, both consciously and unconsciously, to take yourself one step closer. This is then something that will repeat itself over and over again. All of a sudden, you will realize that you are doing what was on the action board: visiting the places, working the way you wanted to, being with the kind of people you wished for, and maybe carrying the bag of your dreams (if that was your dream). It happens because you know where you want to be, the brain feels safe, and you have released the "how" to the universe.

To get you started, I suggest you pick up magazines and brochures from friends, family, and old bookstores and maybe let some unexpected happenings affect your search. You want to have a mix of magazines and material you know and material you don't know because I want you to be open to finding answers in unexpected places and use your gut feeling.

While you will be using the next few days to collect material, I want you to be open to the unexpected. The answer to your question is rarely where you expect it to be.

Exercise No. 10:

- Make a conscious decision and set an intention of welcoming the unexpected.
- Spend the next couple of days collecting material.
- Let words and pictures speak to you.

♥

I hope you are sitting with a stack of material before you. If you are not, and you think that you will do it later and now you want to get to THE ANSWER of how to become a millionaire, I would like you to reflect on why you bought the book and ask yourself if you are willing to do the work it takes, or if you are going to procrastinate for the rest of your life. If you do not have a stack of material in front of you, please put down the book and come back when you have material in front of you.

♥

So, I am now assuming that you are ready for the change. Good for you. Maybe you have started to cut out stuff because you were inspired. If not, that is also good. Please wait just a few more minutes.

I want to spend a short amount of time reflecting. If you wish, you can take out a piece of paper to write on. If you choose to write on your phone, please start by putting it in flight mode so you leave distractions outside this exercise.

Put your attention to what lights your gut feeling and what you want to do with it. You can look into what your relationships with others should look like or how they should feel. Do you want to travel? What do you want to do for a living? This is a money book, but you can use this technique in all areas of life. Think about how you will spend your time when you are a millionaire.

For me, I spent many years making flows in factories more efficient, and then I started doing healing, which lit a spark in me to pursue my dream of opening a health and wellness center. After opening the health and wellness center, I almost immediately felt I was missing the world of engineers and factories. For a while, I thought I had to choose either my spiritual connection or my intelligent problem-solving passion, but it turned out that what fuels me was a combination. The spiritual part of me is a way of living. It is the core of my being and the foundation of who I am. It allows me to be a better problem solver and a better leader. So, I choose both. What you choose is up to you but focus on what lights your fire. The bags were a symbol for me, is there anything that symbolizes wealth for you?

Think about how you want to work. How many hours do you want to work? What amount do you want to get paid? How much do you want to see in your different accounts? What is the total sum of your assets? How is your boss treating you? Are you a leader? What kind of people do you work with? What kind of machines do you work with?

Write down some notes to guide your visualization of your dreams and goals. Let go of any need to control "the how"; how will I do this? Just focus on the feeling and the outcome. It has to be believable to you. You have to believe that you are worthy of it. Maybe you will cut out words and not even know why. That is totally OK. Let your gut guide you.

Exercise No. 11:

- · Cut out any picture or word that inspires you and that you can see for yourself.
- · Choose your background paper. It can be white or colored. You choose the size that is right for you. I like them big to make a little free space to allow the universe to do magical things. You do size and color in a way that inspires you.
- · Arrange all the images on the board and glue them onto the pepper.
- · Hang your masterpiece in a visible place.

There is no wrong way to do the board, but I believe there is a wrong way to put it up. I have seen friends put their action boards inside the closet, and it just didn't work for them. My belief is that it is because they are signaling to themselves that this is not a dream worthy of daylight. I hang mine in the kitchen. Not only do I see it daily, but all my guests see it, too. It sparks conversations where I make myself accountable for my dream. And more importantly, it sparks conversations about my guest's dreams. I love to hear other people's dreams and dig into the fuel of fire. So, I encourage you to arrange the vision board in a place where you can see it daily.

When you finish your vision board, we will talk more about dedicated work vs. hard work and how a shift in thoughts about work can help you let go of things that drain you. Also, the mind shift can give you a better quality of life and wealth.

♥

Chapter Eight

Dedicated work VS. hard work

This is one of the most important lessons I want you to get. There is a massive difference between getting paid for hard work versus getting paid for dedicated work. Hard work is when you get paid by the hour, and everything depends on you doing a lot of hours. Getting paid for dedicated work is when you get paid for the value you bring to the table. Don't confuse this with your value. Your salary and money in the bank say nothing about your worth, but that is a later chapter. Let's talk about how your time is worth massive compensation.

A job that pays by the hour will never give you that. If you are a nurse, you might get angry with me now and say that you are dedicated to your work and need to get paid for the hours you put in. I totally understand where you are coming from. I think a lot of people think this way. May I be so bold as to say that it is a major reason, they do not have money in the bank at the end of the month?

Let me explain it by giving an example. When I went to programming school, I met a nurse who had attended class the year before me. By going to school for two years, she was offered a job before the third year started because a hospital saw that she could be the perfect link between the IT department and all the doctors and nurses who "ordered" new programs to make their lives easier. From that day, she more than doubled her income and got working hours that were able to give her the comfortable life that she wanted. Today, five years later, she started her own consultancy where she could work even fewer hours and get more paid.

I love this example because it clearly shows how the value, she brings to the table is worth so much more than her time. I am not saying we don't need nurses, but if you want a fat bank account and time to spend with your loved ones, then the nurse in the emergency room can be someone other than you. You have the power to change your path in a direction that gives you more wealth, time, and happiness than you could ever dream of.

If you think you have to be great from the beginning in this new direction, you are letting your past beliefs and thoughts shape your reality. Are you using a fear or illusion as an excuse to stop you? let me tell you: honestly, I am not the best coder. Actually, I barely passed the class. One time, I almost cried in school from the frustration of just not getting the lessons, but I didn't give up. I kept the focus on getting to my highest potential and found a small niche where I rocked it, and from there, I could grow, and so can you.

Sometimes you have to team up with someone else to work up the courage to do what you desire to do. It was like that for me back in 2019. I had been accepted into school and had held the live event, which was seen by more than 2000 people. I now knew in my gut that I had a purpose: helping people raise their vibration by combining the 'fluffy stuff' and science.

Writing intentions and gratitude almost daily was part of my routine. I had several different notebooks lying around the house, but still there never seemed to be a good place to keep track of it. So, I started writing in my old calendar.

I use a physical calendar for several different reasons: it calms me to turn the pages, helps me maintain an overview of larger periods, and serves as an archive, like a diary.

At the beginning of the year, I map out major astrological events for my zodiac sign and add them to my calendar. I do this to heighten awareness of recurring patterns from the past and to leverage positive energy when the timing is right.

I am not an astrologer, but it has fascinated me my whole life. I follow different astrologers, and over time have found those that I can relate to. I find that many astrologers will spend many words explaining the astrology happening, but few words on what that means for me.

I was missing a calendar where I could write my intention for the day, and my gratitude in the evening but also had knowledge of major astrological events so I reached out to a calendar publisher and started to create that calendar. The amount of money it would cost me to print scared me. Remember I was still a student, and didn't have any money in the bank.

One day, I had one of those feelings I described before, that gut instinct telling me this was something I had to do. I took inspired action and reached out to one of the astrologers I was following, asking her if she would collaborate on creating the calendar with me. My intention was for her to explain celestial events, and for me to articulate how to best harness that energy.

It was divine timing; she told me that people often reached out to her to co-create, but she had so far turned down every offer. Lately, she had been thinking about making a calendar but didn't know how to bring it to fruition.

We talked about her desires and intentions for the calendar she had in mind. I was willing to make some changes in this first version, but not all of them. We found some good compromises and were ready to order.

We both believed we could sell 2000 calendars and make some money, but there was a risk that we wouldn't sell any. I told her that I would share the winnings equally with her if she would share the risk equally with me. We went over different scenarios we could think of, and then she agreed. I still didn't know where to find the money for the advance payment of the publication, but I trusted the universe, my gut feeling and stayed open to unexpected events.

Only days after laying the order, I received a notice from the IRS that I would get money back on my taxes from last year. There had been a miscommunication when I worked at the spa and the money I would get back, was exactly the amount I needed for the advance payment for the calendar. So again, it all worked out magically.

We did sell all 2000 copies, not all of them at full price, but it was enough money to cover my payments for the old engagements that I was still dragging along from the health and wellness center. I had enough and I was more than happy to share half with her.

We parted ways after that first calendar. She wanted to do one on her own that was in her style, and I wanted to continue with the format that I had come to love. We still talk frequently, and both share a common respect. We acknowledged that neither of us would have made a calendar without the other. I am forever grateful for our collaboration.

As I said before, one purpose of the book is to shift your focus from who you were yesterday, with the beliefs you had yesterday, into the person you are today, with the beliefs of who you can become tomorrow by being it today. By believing it today. Just set the intention, be open to listening to your gut, and take inspired action.

A solution to a desire rarely turns out how you have imagined it, BUT it turns out so much better if you know how to set an intention. A writer friend, Camilla, was low on cash but didn't want to give up her desire to write her next book. She made a pledge to herself that she would be writing her next book while still being able to support her family. It was clear what she wanted; she had set her intention. A few days later, she was offered a job as a personal assistant. The person she worked for had a daily routine of seeing certain TV shows in the middle of the day and didn't mind if Camilla was writing her book simultaneously. Suddenly, she found that she was paid for her time while writing. The universe finds these amazing miracles and ways of delivering what you want if you are open to following the guidance that you receive.

I will give you one of my favorite affirmations, and I will also be giving you an exercise. This affirmation has helped me shift my thoughts about myself and the worth of my work. It is partly inspired by Amanda Frances and incorporated into the Miracle calendar I have published for the last four years.

Exercise No. 12:

· Read the affirmation repeatedly until you believe it is true.

· Put it up in a place where you can see it every day, so it becomes your new truth.

♥

I am thankful and open to meeting people who help me on my journey in the right direction for my highest good. I prepare and position myself for financial growth through the way I:

♥ Spend ♥ Save ♥ Donate ♥
♥ Share ♥ Invest ♥
♥ Receive and Generate Money ♥

I am moving into new levels of recurring revenue and abundance. The universe spreads its generosity upon me, and I receive it with gratitude now. Gold is showering upon me. I receive money and gifts from expected and unexpected places. I am worthy of this. I am a place for growth, happiness, and abundance. I love myself and honor myself. The universe supports my heartfelt work, and I get paid manifold for my services. In this moment, I am the creator. I am the source. I am grateful. I am.

♥

With this affirmation, I intend to increase my vibration to take myself to the next level of conciseness. I write my affirmations in different places, to lift different types of energy throughout the day. I have some printed in the Mirical calendar, some I write on my bathroom mirror, and others on the inside of my closet. These gentle reminders impact my state of mind, raise my vibration, and guide me in the right direction.

Wealth can come from three diffrent directions: You can inherit it; you can create it through business and wise investments or you can win the lottery. In a way, you attract in all three situations, but your expectations might be different, and therefore the energy and frequency you send out to the universe will be different.

My friend Rolf won 3 million dollars through the lottery back in 2011. The feeling was surrealist and hard to grasp. It didn't become real until the week after when he was reading the paper and looking at housing advertising and realized that he could buy whatever he wanted.

In the months leading up to the win, two things happened. First, he cut back on his gambling. He had been gambling on horses but felt that he no longer had the time to read up on facts and was losing money. So he quit gambling on horses. Second, he started winning small amounts more often on scratch-off tickets and the lottery. He could feel a shift in the energy. It's hard for him to explain, but it was exciting in a different way. He was in a flow, and expecting to win, and he did.

Like most lottery players I know, Rolf had also played with the thought of what he would do if he won, but reality was very different. "You must be happy now?" a colleague had asked him, but Rolf explained that happiness doesn't come with money. The freedom to not worry about paying bills is a good feeling, but it is not happiness. Helping kids with a down payment for a house gives him joy, but it is not happiness. He is not happier now than he was before. He has more freedom and that decreased stress because he knows he is free to make other choices like taking a taxi for longer distances if the car breaks down. More freedom gives less, but it is not happiness. He thinks people often confuse freedom with happiness.

He reflects a lot about happiness and finds that spending time with his kids is happiness for him. He can look at people in love and imagine that waking up next to someone that you love must be happiness. Often people commend on how he spends the money or ask why he doesn't travel more. For Rolf it doesn't make sense to travel alone, he would like to share the experience.

His spending hasn't changed; sure, the suit might be handmade in Italy and made out of silk, but the shirt he is wearing on the day of the interview is low-budget. He still compares prices and shops for groceries at cheaper places. For him, it makes no sense to pay more for the same loaf of bread, at a different store.

Before winning, he would spend extra on ecological food and food from small farms, and this is one area where the spending has increased. Other than that, he thinks that he has stayed the same. He gives three reasons for this: first, there was a system set up around winning large amounts of money with several coaching sessions. Second, he kept his job for another year and a half, and third, Rolf was lucky to receive mentorship from an old friend who had sold his own company years before.

The mentorship meant a lot to Rolf. They had conversations as often as once a month, for several years. It could be about what bank to use and who to talk to. The best advice, or maybe warning he got from his mentor was that he shouldn't lose his footing because he would never get it back.

His gambling is at the same level as before. He still plays the same coupon and has the same excitement every week. He still drives around in the same old car and not much has changed. When he won his money he attracted a large sum at one. I created my wealth over time. I am looking forward to you telling me how it played out in your life.

Going through transformation, one part is emotional healing, and the other is monetary growth. In the next chapter, I will share some concrete tips that can change how you view the economic field and create an increase.

♥

Chapter Nine

Creating wealth
out of nothing

When I was on rock bottom, a friend of a friend committed suicide when it became known that he had filed for bankruptcy. I won't pretend to know what was in his head, but research shows that those rescued from suicide attempts say that it is not that they wanted to die; they just didn't want to feel the way they were feeling.

I know that I had deep feelings of guilt, failure, and shame when I was at my lowest. My beliefs about myself got shaken to the ground. I doubted if I was as bright as I had believed and if my trust in others was too naive. I doubted beliefs I had known to be true for a long time. Ultimately, I had two choices: to give up or start creating my life. I choose creation.

Another person who chose the creation of wealth is my friend Helena Svensson, known on Instagram as miljonarmamman. I think you will be as fascinated and inspired by her story as I was, and let me tell you upfront you are in the perfect position to do what she did right now. Helena created millions of Swedish crowns from the dark place of having nothing.

In the middle of the financial crisis in 2008, she and her husband lived on a bare minimum, with a tiny baby to support. She was unemployed but received a small amount of parental leave benefit. Her husband contributed by working some hours here and there. Eight years later, she was a Swedish millionaire. Let me repeat: from almost no income, no savings, flat broke, to millionaire in eight years.

She started her Instagram account to share how she did it. Her vibration was tuned into "If I can do it, anyone can do it." She often points out that you do not need a Master's degree in economics or a lot of starting capital to get started. You just need to get started and stick to some simple principles. Well, the principles are simple; it is sticking to them that can be tricky. But she has good advice for that as well.

For her, it all started with her stumbling upon Per H. Børjssons book "This is How All Swedes Can Become Millionaires." Although she and her husband had nothing to spare, she bought the book anyway, hoping for a change in her life.

The book's main idea is that you should save 10% of your salary each month before you do anything else with the money. Her problem was she did not have 10%

to save. She had nothing. They were broke. However, the book made her reflect upon how to create a surplus. She liked the idea of having a surplus instead of just surviving from month to month.

No matter if you are unemployed, earning $ 2,000 or $ 20,000 per month, it is very common that it is all gone by the end of the month. Science has shown that there is no correlation between how much you earn and how much you are saving. In other words, it is normal for humans to spend all we have every month unless we become aware of our spending habits and how they affect our future. Today, you can make new choices in handling your income, savings, donations, spending, and investments.

Helena got a job at the local supermarket and started working on the weekends. She knew they had survived on what they had before, so she decided to save her entire salary. That was her first step. She was increasing the inflow of money and saving it.

She had never bought a stock. She did not know the stock market, but she followed the book's advice because it rang true to her. She believed this was the right way to increase her wealth and was willing to be patient.

She points out that she feels lucky that it was in the middle of the financial crisis when she started investing. Many stocks were close to their lowest point ever; therefore, their value increased faster than expected, and the increase was steeper than expected. However, she also explains that, at the time, it didn't feel easy because the media was full of bleeding stories about how this was the end of the world. The rally at the stock market was long gone, and her parents were upset with her. They thought she was foolish to invest money in a stock market that kept going down and down. They felt she was wasting money she didn't have to spare. Remember, she was still only working on the weekends and had difficulty making ends meet.

Eventually, she got a full-time job and adjusted the strategy accordingly.

Her top three tips for financial freedom are:

1. Pay yourself first every month. 10% is a good estimate, but if you are not mentally there, focus on creating a higher income than your spending. Turn it around and spend less than your income, which is easier if you already have paid yourself.
2. Dare to invest in the stock market. You do not have to be an expert. You do not have to handpick stocks. You are allowed to be a beginner, and you are allowed to choose funds that are made up of a wide variety of stocks and have low charges.
3. Give it time. It should be a little bit boring. If it is exciting, you are chasing kicks, and your focus is in the wrong place.

♥

Companies pay out a portion of their earnings to shareholders regularly, similar to how banks pay you interest rates. This is called a dividend and is paid out in the form of cash or additional stock. The dividend allows you to take advantage of the principle of compound interest. You need time to get the most out of compound interest, so give it time. It is **time** that creates abundance.

Helena's initial goal was to become a Swedish millionaire and feel financially free. That goal has changed. There was a shift from dreaming of having financial freedom to dreaming of feeling financially secure. It went from being about the money invested to the feeling of security on a cellular level in her body. For her, that meant knowing that her finances could stand another recession. She wanted to be confident she could go on vacation, even in a new recession. She wanted to sleep well at night, not worrying about the effects of a new recession.

Now, this time around, when we are going into a recession or expecting some recession, she looks at the market slightly differently. Even though we do not know how long this period will be, she has a different view of this crisis than the last one. The one in 2008 was a crash; this one seems more controlled, at least initially. Now, a lot has changed in the last year, and as always, we do not know the future.

We have a similar opportunity now to buy under-valued stocks in some markets, as Helena did in 2008. The key learnings she took away from 2008 were:

> What you buy at a discounted price during the recession when most companies are undervalued needs a shorter period to reach a good result, compared to a stock purchased overvalued. Note that not all stocks are undervalued during a recession, and not all stocks are overvalued when there is a rally in the stock market.

The book's author, who had inspired Helena years before, saw her account on Instagram. He liked her work and offered her a job at his investment company. Helena thought it would be a fun job to grow into. She is now surrounded by some people who do not have to work but still choose to do so.

Something exciting happens in the body when you do not need to work to survive but can choose to work with what you think is the most fun work.

This is also true in my experience. When money is no longer the main object, but you work for fun and purpose, work brings joy to life. That doesn't mean that there aren't any challenges or that life doesn't go up and down. It simply means that one's mind is open to a different perception of what it means to work. I genuinely believe we can all create that illusion and that it is not tied to money; it is merely linked to our perception of what is possible for ourselves. We can create a happy illusion about why we work and what work brings to our lives.

Research shows that when people sell their life's work and make a fortune, they often feel empty and sad. Some say they lose the feeling of purpose in life and have to recreate it in new ways. Again, after a certain point, there is no correlation between money and happiness. Happiness is something you create internally by clearing out all of the old shit that is in the way. On the other hand, you can have both happiness and a shit load of money, and that is what I want for you.

Helena explains that in the journey of healing her relationship with money and creating abundance, her goal has shifted from having a Swedish million in the stock account to building financial security. She hasn't changed the way she saves; it looks the same, but her income has increased, so therefore her savings and spending have increased.

If you want to save money each month, that is an active choice and something you must decide about. Possibly, you need to change patterns and beliefs about money and your potential accomplishments.

♥

"Can you rethink? Of course, you can. The real question is, are you willing to?"

Exercise No. 13:

- Free write for 10 minutes about what thoughts occurred while reading her story. Think of at least three places where you can cut costs and at least three places where you can increase your income. It is allowed to be crazy, fun, and full of imagination.
- When you are done writing, let these thoughts land with you. Is there anything in there that is possible for you to start doing?
- How would your month change if you saved 10% of your income at the beginning of the month?
- How would you feel if your stock account increased every month?

One part of increasing wealth is how you save and invest your money; another is how you look at your assets and what you have today.

♥

Although she has a lot of money, Helena often talks about appreciating the small things. She explains that feeling appreciation and thankfulness for the small things is a superpower. She points out that if you are not satisfied with where you are now, you will not be satisfied with where you are in a year from now or where you are when you have that million in the bank. Like Rolf explained it, happiness comes in the interaction with the people you love and has nothing to do with money.

In her youth, Helena travelled around the world, often to countries with a lot of poverty. She noticed that in those countries, more people were very grateful for what they had. In contrast to the more industrialized countries in today's world, where more and more people have lost their ability to appreciate the small things in life.

To keep focus on gratitude, Helena has a morning meditation routine. She starts her meditation with a body scan, where she directs her focus of attention to different parts of the body, from the toes through her body and up to her head. The purpose is to create awareness. She ends her morning routine with thoughts of gratitude. Just like I do, she finds at least three areas of her life that she is grateful for that morning. It helps to keep peace of mind and avoid any hasty decisions and jumping into tempting "too good to be true" offers.

Helena and I end the interview with concluding that you can always find excuses to spend money. There are so many things in life we think we need, but it is good to take a step back and evaluate why we are consuming.

Whit that said, I am all for buying what makes you feel good. Let me tell you that it is possible to spend, save, invest, and donate all at the same time. It is all a flow of money, where you give it away, and it returns. Sometimes, you need to keep it with you for a little longer, and sometimes you need to invest immediately. You will know what is right for you.

You have worked for what you have; now, let it work for you. Money flows so easily when creation comes from pure intention and is followed up by inspired actions, and that is what I will guide you through in the next chapter.

♥

Chapter Ten

Creating from pure intention and inspired action

As I told you earlier, an intention is a conscious decision to focus on a particular goal or outcome. Pure intention is when the intention is created from a place of love. Pure love is where you feel connected to your higher self and the rest of the universe. It is a place where you can see how your contribution matters to the world.

Sometimes, I will meditate before getting to that state. Other times, I can get there by having conversations with great friends or a coach. One time, I woke up from a dream where I was meditating on the top of a mountain and felt the purest love I had ever felt. It was so pure that a tear fell down my cheeks as I woke up. I was so humble in front of this beauty and pureness. This is a place I like to visit in meditation. Going there helps me let go of my Ego; it centers me and helps me feel how I contribute to making the world a better place. Here, I can create from a truly pure intention.

There are a lot of different guided meditations out there that can help you get to your center and connect you to your higher self. If you want a more active approach, I love the power pose, where I stand with my legs apart and my arms wide open, and I say my intention. Let's do it together.

Exercise No. 14:

- Stand up with your legs and arms wide open.
- Look up toward the sky to get a deeper connection to the Source.
- Say and feel: "I am open for love to flow through me and be of higher service".
- Say and feel: "It is safe for me to be a channel".
- Say and feel: "Only good will come from this experience".
- Feel the feelings that occur in your body.
- Repeat whenever you need to lift your energy.

♥

When I have workshops or talks, I will do this exercise several times through the session because it always clears some blockage and helps us get back to the pure knowledge we all have within. I often do the exercise before writing or creating course content. It is a good exercise to do before we create and take inspired actions.

Creating from pure intention is an inspired action. When you draw on a canvas, Dance, put words on paper, or whatever is creative for you, that is exactly the creation it needs to be. Inspired actions can also be making a phone call, writing an email, or knocking on the door of a stranger.

When you connect Source and feel that anything is possible, anything is possible. When you are open to being of higher service and know that you are safe, new ideas may spark in you. This is the place where you attract amazing happenings. An inspired action is when you connect your gut feeling, a sudden idea with an action in the real world. It is a place where you allow yourself to feel maybe a little discomfort because you need to be brave in a way you haven't been before.

Exercise No. 15:

- Know in your heart that you are safe and only good will come of this.
- Think of one inspired action that you could do right now to get you one step closer to your dream.
- Do it.

- Feel the feelings that are in your body afterward.
- Write down some words of your bravery and how you feel right now.

♥

Connecting to sources and taking inspired actions is something I do every day. It didn't start like that, but over the years of practice, I have received so many proofs that it cannot be ignored. In the waken state, it is the best way to get energy moving and attracting my desires.

Let's start to connect all the bits and pieces that you have gathered throughout the book and make it into one beautiful puzzle. When you heal your past beliefs about money and start trusting your gut feeling, you can listen to that inner voice and properly get ideas that feel crazy or unfamiliar, and that is okay. Go with that thought, do that inspired action that is waiting to happen. You will be amazed by the outcome. I promise. I also promise that it will never look how you think it will; it will look better.

This is why you can't set your goals or intentions for a specific person. When you do that, you are chasing instead of attracting. Chasing energy will push you further away. The reason behind that is that the core emotion of that is lack.

The universe is smarter than you and can make up better solutions than you can ever imagine, so instead of saying, "I will receive a raise from my boss" or "This client will pay me double," you can reformulate to " I am open for a raise or a higher flow of income from known or unknown sources." There are two major differences; one is that the first sentence talks about something happening in the future, meaning lack today. Also, they were specific, which will narrow down the possibilities of the universe to deliver. The second sentence is in the present; It is at this moment that you are open for receiving, and it can come from anywhere, so the possibilities are endless. If there is only one takeaway that you will get from this book, this is the lesson that has surprised me the most and also has given me the most.

Sometimes, it happens instantly. I literally have a thought, and two seconds later, I meet that person, or that check arrives in the mailbox. Other times, it takes the source a little while to rearrange according to my new standards. I call this the time in between.

I encourage you to trust the process. You can compare it to planting a seed. Let's compare the journey between planting a tomato and a potato. I am not an expert in either, but I have done it for some years. Bear with me if I oversimplify. When planting a tomato, you quickly see the results of the process. The timespan from you putting the seed in the ground until you see something green coming out of the ground is a matter of days if you give it the correct amount of water, warmth, and light. Now, when you set a potato in the ground, it takes months before the blast starts to show itself, and when it does, you are supposed to cover it with more soil so it can become even stronger. It is like recognizing that it is happening, but it is not quite ready to be on your plate.

In neither of the processes do you dig into the ground to uncover the seed to see how it is growing. Your job is simply to have trust and create the perfect environment around you. It is the same with your dream and intention. You plant it, and then you give it good conditions. If your dream is to become a millionaire, there are some good conditions or steps you can take to position yourself better:

- Healing past relationship with money.
- Changing the view of what you are worthy of having.
- Education.
- Mentorship.
- Change of job.
- Saving in the stock market.
- Investing in houses.
- Any of the steps you saw for yourself in the freewriting exercises.
- Any of the emotions you channel in the action board creation.
- Create recurring revenue (is also one I will come back to later).

All of those are different ways of watering your seeds.

♥

Sometimes, you have to add an extra year of education, just like the potato needs more soil to become stronger and bigger. Sometimes, the conditions are perfect; instead of rein, the sun is out to shine on the tomato, and it gets ripped faster, and you can cut a year of education. That was what happened to me. I didn't need to do the last year of programming because the opportunity occurred earlier.

We do not know the way in advance, and that is not our job. For you, Your job is to plant the seed, water it, and give it love and nourishment. Trust the process. Set the goals of where you want to go and leave "the how" up to the universe.

In your body, know the difference between planting the seed, the time in between, and when the time is right.

Exercise No. 16:

- Take out your journal or your freewriting tool.
- Reflect on a recent event where you set a seed, like doing the vision board or signing up for a class. What did that feel like?
- What did it feel like when the seed was in the ground, the wait, the trust? Do you often search for signs of growth, or do you trust?
- What does it feel like in the body when you can pick a ripe tomato because the time is right? When in your life have you experienced that?

· What can you do to water your dreams and give them nourishment and sunlight?

♥

Just buying this book is a way to tell you subconscious that you are ready to attract money and gifts. It is a way of healing your old money wounds, watering your dreams, and creating wealth for yourself and those around you. And yes, I literally mean that when you start creating wealth for yourself, it will affect those around you. When you put your focus on creating wealth from pure intentions, magic happens.

The universe is smarter than you. The universe is more creative than you. The universe is an infinity of possibilities, and therefore, you should not limit yourself when creating. I have already said it a couple of times, but I have seen it so many times that it cannot be said enough. Your job is to set the "what" and let the universe fix the "how." No matter what I am affirming, there is one sentence I always add, and I want you to add this to your daily thoughts. Whatever you create, you want to add "from expected or unexpected places, like this or even better" because what you wish for can come from so many other places than you think of. Let me give you some examples:

One of my followers on Instagram, Jenny Meyer, wished for new socks one day because the ones she had were worn out. The next day, she bought a dresser from a second-hand store. When she came home, she discovered three pairs of new socks in the right size in the middle drawer. Another time, one week, she went into a designer store dreaming of one of the jackets; the next week, she found it at a second-hand store and got it for 1/10 of the price.

For me, the largest financial shift happened in the strangest week of my life. Let me tell you how the universe had put hurdles in the way to lead me onto my perfect path. Leading up to what was both one of my happiest weeks and the saddest of my life, I had studied programming for two years and had one year left. In the spring of 2021, my mom had become sick with cancer. Even though the doctor had given her a good prognosis, I had a bad feeling. In school, I could only focus on one of the classes. My head could not handle the work of two new subjects, and I failed the class I never attended. In the summer, I got a letter from the government that I would not receive any more loans or funding for school before I had a passing grade in all subjects. I received a letter from the school that I was not admitted into the fall classes. They had reassessed my classes from years earlier and no longer judged them as high as earlier, so I was no longer admitted to the Masterclasses. To me, this was so strange; I had been in tight dialog for two years to ensure I did everything right. I screamed at the universe, "What do you want me to do." I thought it was unfair that

I had given up the life I knew to return to school for two years just for this to happen. I did not understand it.

The choice of going back to school never felt like a choice; it felt like an order from my stomach, and still, here I was without finance and without enrollment. It felt like I failed again, even though I knew in my heart that I had done the right thing. I screamed and cried and went to bed exhausted. The next day, I had an email notification about a former colleague posting a job on LinkedIn. In the two years I was in school, I had stayed away from LinkedIn. I didn't want to get distracted and lured back into "old jobs" just to satisfy my financial wishes, but this morning, I got curious.

My work colleague had called me a couple of weeks earlier about a job he wanted me to take. I explained where I was in the process, and that kind of job belonged to the old me. We discussed where I was heading, and he informed me that within a couple of months, there would be an opening in his company for a better-paid job closer to my new wishes.

I was excited when I followed the link to see what job he had posted. Just reading the heading, I saw that this was not the job for me. I remember thinking, "Universe, why did you want me to go here if this is what I get?" but then my eyes fell to the next post. It was my dream job. This was the job I had gone back to school for. This was a job I always knew had to exist but had never seen on display before.

I knew this job was a perfect match for me, and it turned out that I had met the recruiter years earlier in another setting, so it was really easy for me to give him a call and ask questions about the job. He encouraged me to apply and said he would get back to me after the summer vacation.

This is when we arrive at the strangest week. I was called to an interview. I was prepared, and it went well. I thought they would call me back for a second interview.

I remember telling my mom. She expressed joy. She was excited for me, or the way it is with some grandparents; I think she was most excited about my children having a mother with an income. She never understood why I had left the career I had to start the health and wellness center that almost went bankrupt. Even more, she didn't understand why I would go back to school when I had no money instead of going back to well-paid jobs. She had many times over the years expressed her concern for my children and my finances. She was afraid that I would not give them a good life. Discussions about the lessons of following your heart and enjoying free adventures never really rang true to her, but for this, she was happy.

Two days later, she passed unexpectedly in the middle of the night. It was a shock to my family and friends. The treatment had been working very well. I read the whole journal afterward, and the doctors had made progress and examined every possibility. It was just the way of life.

In all of my sorry, I received a phone call for the second interview. I explained what had happened and that I would not be in the best of shape for an interview, but they assured me that they were a company where you were allowed to be human, and they would take it into account.

The HR person told me that he would bring another person with a similar job into the meeting, not to figure out my weaknesses but to find my areas of strength so they could put me in the right context for onboarding if we got that far. I didn't believe him. My past experiences are all about HR being very interested in your weaknesses and the lessons you learned. But this was a different company. In the interview, they truly cared about my goals and how they could use my experience in the best way possible.

That week changed my life. Both emotionally and financially. Feeling incredibly happy and really sad at the same time made me understand more about what I was capable of feeling.

Financially, when I summed up the first year of work, I saw that my salary, pension, bonuses, compensation fees, and with the currency effect, I arrived at a seven-figure number for the second time in my life. It was a huge milestone. When I combined that with some money that my mom had left me, I started to invest, donate, and spend more money.

Having this financial freedom changed how I radiated. I had proven to myself what my bankrupt self knew I could accomplish. People were paying me for the value of my knowledge, and it felt good.

Strangers stared to treat me differently. When I walk into a hotel with my Louis Vuittons', the receptionists are kinder than when I come with my old luggage. Some of it is because of their beliefs, and some of it is because of the energy I send out. That feeling of being my new rich me, I want to give that to you without you having to lose a parent or failing in school.

♥

Chapter Eleven

Feeling financially free, abundant, and value the new you

Your salary and money in the bank say nothing about your value. Even if I loved the moment I could buy those first Vuitton's, I also reflect on the outer appearances we put upon ourselves as a shell to protect us from showing who we really are. No matter how we dress or what car we drive, we are still together with that voice in our head 24-7. That voice will tell you what you have trained it to.

I would love for you to embrace the unique value you bring to the world and have the feeling of being free and abundant. I want you to know that everything that is meant for you is already making its way towards you.

The law of purpose is one of the Universal laws that say that we exist to fulfill a purpose. I believe that when we are in contact with our gut feelings, we are free to create that purpose the way we wish to. Most of this book is centered around you coming in contact with your sacred self and embodying it how you want to.

Numerous studies show that we feel a sense of belonging when we have a strong social connection and relationship with family, friends, and communities. We strive to feel this from when we are newborns; that is why we mimic everyone else. We want to belong so that if danger comes, we will be protected and survive. It feels good to be around like-minded people. I believe we are here on earth to have experiences and to learn. We need other people to do that. It is in the interaction that we grow.

Pursuing personal goals, learning, and growing brings a sense of accomplishment and a sense of purpose. It doesn't matter if it is career-related, educational, or related to personal growth. For me, going back to school to get a specific type of job was a goal. I have always used education as a sidekick in life to help me grow. I love setting foot on campus. It makes me happy to surround myself with people who know more than me. Also, it gives me the feeling that possibilities are endless.

It's important to note that the sources of purpose and meaning in life can be different for you. Just because school provides value and meaning for me, it may not have that effect on you.

In this next exercise, I want you to focus on what makes you happy. Focus on the last time you felt happiness.

Exercise No. 17:

Give examples and write down the last time you were happy in these different situations:

- Together with family or friends.
- Together with your community.
- Engaged in acts of kindness.
- Pursued a personal goal.
- In a spiritual or religious setting.
- From growth and learning something new.
- From purchasing something.
- From giving something away.
- From cleaning.
- From eating healthy.
- From pleasure.
- From any other situation.

What were you most connected to? Is there anywhere where you feel more fulfilled? Does any of it give a sense of purpose or meaning in life? Are there any areas that you would like to explore more?

♥

The money itself didn't make me happy, but I took the opportunity to make positive new stories in all areas of life along the way. I created self-worth from within, and from that, I could create new, unique, happy moments. Because that is what it is all about creating those brief instances of an elusive state of being intertwined with joy.

When creating your new you, happiness and money are available to you. You get to decide what makes you happy. It is the same with abundance. There are many different areas of life where we can feel abundance. In this book, I want to focus on the feeling of abundance of Money.

The nervous system relaxes when we feel we have enough or more than enough money. For me, there are two feelings I always come back to. The first one is the feeling of going to the grocery store and being able to buy whatever my heart desires in the quality I wish for. That symbolizes total freedom and abundance to me. What I did, and still do, is that while walking in the store, I will tell myself that I can buy whatever I wish. I also talk to myself about all the good deals that are in my path.

Another routine that has been with me for a long time is the feeling of being happy to pay my bills. I do thankfulness while I am paying. So, I literally talk to my bills: "Thank you, mortgage, for giving me a roof over my head. Thank you, electricity company, for giving me light in my house. Thank you, hockey club, for providing my son with a safe and fun place to hang, exercise, and learn ".

When connecting gratitude to the result of spending money, abundance appears because the value is enlarged. Connection small things to larger things and eventually realizing that everything is connected is the greatest gift you can give yourself.

Abundance is a mindset. It's a perspective that focuses on the richness of life itself rather than the lack of resources. Financial wealth is undoubtedly a part of abundance, but it's only a fraction of the equation. Abundance, in its fullest sense, embraces an inner sense of prosperity, and fulfillment.

Exercise No. 18:

Journal and elaborate on:

- Could you be thankful for bills and other expenses in a way you have not been before?
- Where in your life do you see that you have enough?
- Can you expand that into other areas?

♥

I love that feeling when you have seen proof that you can create, you know it is true. For me, I am fascinated by how fast you can build or rebuild wealth. I am also fascinated with how quickly you can spend it.

Did you know that a high percentage of lottery winners lose it all again within a few years? Some even end up losing more than they won. When you have money, some people around you will expect you to pay for them. Some will try to scam you. If you want, you can put a lot of fear into the emotion of being rich, but let's focus on trust.

♥

Chapter Twelve

Leverage - Keeping it and getting more

Leverage is another of my favorite words, it means that you strategically use a tool or advantage to enhance your effectiveness or influence, like gaining a positive impact through well-placed effort. One example is investing in the stock market another is the year and a half I spent writing this book. The time I invest is a way for me to help more people than I ever could in one-to-one coaching. A chapter on leverage is to get you to think of how and why you spend, both money and time.

It is so easy to think that a small SMS loan won't hurt or that you need that coffee daily on your way to work. Or why not get a brand-new car when everyone in the neighborhood is getting one?

Writing a whole chapter on how to cut expenses seems boring to me. It is not the way I live myself, so I would be lying if I would be recommending it. I think that you should spend money and feel excited about spending. Feel good about it and spend them mindfully. You should borrow money if it makes sense to you. I have taken loans to create a base for good investments.

Do you know Ingvar Kamprad? He was the founder of IKEA. Sadly he passed away a couple of years ago. Even after being very wealthy, he would still drive around in his old Volvo V70. I think it is funny that both Millionaire Rolf and I also drive around in old Volvo V70 cars.

It is no secret that a new car is always a bad financial investment, but if it makes you feel good every time you drive it, it is a good emotional investment and worth it. For me, the old Volvo is more about my inability to find a new car that can fit as much in the trunk and still be cheap to drive.

You might wonder why it has to be cheap to drive if I have enough money to make a different choice. So far, I find it more rewarding to invest, travel, and donate. That might change when I acknowledge the lack of new technology like preheating the car on a snowy winter morning, playlists, or navigation systems, but I am not quite there yet. It is all about choices. What might be right for me might not be right for you, but I do genuinely believe that when it comes to money, we can both have it and spend it and that we should spend it on whatever makes us feel good and support our dreams.

There are two proven ways that you can keep what you have manifested and that you can receive more: One, do your daily meditation, manifestation, and affirmation practice, and two, put yourself in front of new opportunities and take inspired actions. It is that simple. Once you have daily practice routines, it becomes natural to do annual routines that carry over for the rest of your life. It is a continuous cycle of cleaning out old habits and fears to create new wishes and make room to receive what is to come.

Intention, inspired action, and momentum are some other favorite words of mine. Setting the intention for the day, the year, or even the decade will help steer you in the right direction.

I still stumble and fall from time to time. When that happens, I slow down, return to my exercises, and focus on what is important to me. That is how I get back on track. If I am stuck, I ask Source to use me as a tool to help others. This helps me co-create my life.

When you start to receive money, gifts, and new opportunities, it is natural to begin to think about how you should spend, save, invest, and donate. I never was much of a saver if we talked about the traditional way in a bank account with low interest rates. I save short-term as a backup, but my focus is on finding the sweet spot diverting risks like, different stock markets, as well as investing in my company.

Initially, investing in the company meant investing in me or ideas I thought would be fun. Besides being employed full-time, I have had a company or two on the side for about twenty years to play out my hobbies. Sure, I made some money here and there, but I also lost money here and there, like financially failing at building the health and wellness center. All of my investments have been worthwhile because of the lessons I learned. Finally, one day, it hit me; I saw a pattern. I had always been willing to put money into the business, play around different hobbies, and learn new business lessons. However, I had never set the intention of making money long-term.

It can hurt when you have insight because you know you can't continue the same way as before. I got scared that I would no longer be able to focus on the fun part of business, but the universe calmed me down and got me back on track and in the training zone of daily practice.

I can have fun, learn new stuff, and make money all at the same time. I have enough knowledge to make that happen. I have shifted my focus to recurring revenue. Recurring revenue is like compound interest and dividends, an action that happens repeatedly and gives you money each time. Compound interest is the interest that the bank pays you. It can be explained as if you haven't removed any of the money from last year, the bank will pay you interest both on the money you initially put in the bank, but they will also pay you interest on the interest they gave you last year. So, if you save 100 dollars in a savings account and your interest is 10%, the bank will give you 10 dollars in interest the first year.

Now, you have 110 dollars in your account. 10% on that, year two, is 11 dollars, so now you have 121 dollars in your bank account. In year three, they will give you 12,1 dollars because you get 10% of 121 dollars, and so on. This is compound interest.

In the stock market, it is the same procedure; the company will distribute its earnings back to you as a shareholder as a way of saying thanks for loaning them the money. Often, that money will be invested right back into the company, and you now own more shares than you did before. The major difference between investing in the banks with saving accounts and the stock market is that over time, your shares in the stock market will most likely also increase in value, making it a better investment over time.

Recurring revenue is similar in the way that it occurs again and again. For me, that means creating a best-selling book and a workbook with online matching courses. It also means diving into new technology like machine learning and AI and creating NFTs that make me an income every time they are sold. For you, it might be music or something different. Only you can create your future, and I encourage you to do it from your gut.

When you can feel the new you, when you can feel your future today, it is easy to take the first inspired steps. In this book, you have reflected on who your future you is and how it feels to be your future self today. You have taken the first step to attracting wealth. Can you feel that it is already yours?

Maybe you have already noticed changes after doing your exercises throughout this book. Where have you healed the past by making up new stories and illusions? Did unexpected things start to happen? How much money, gifts, and pleasant surprises have shown up?

Let's do one last exercise together.

Exercise No. 19:

- Feel all the good stuff that has happened while reading this book. Please make a list of it.
- Keep your list in a place where it will remind you of what you are capable of creating in such a short amount of time.
- What is an inspired action you can do today that will make you become a new you in the present?
- You already have the knowledge you need to get what is truly yours, so do this last exercise now.

♥

Go "Crown yourself," as Cara Alwill says. It is all about you allowing yourself to call yourself what you want to be. If it is being an Author that is your dream, then talk about yourself as an author, and then slowly let the world know in a manner that feels safe to you. If you want others to believe in you, you must decide what you believe about yourself. Trust yourself; you got this. The new you are here already, and thank you for trusting me throughout the process.

I am truly blessed that you would do so. Keep up the practice, and you will see how the speed increases from when you think of a thought of manifestation until it happens in your life. Momentum is when the vibration around your money thoughts changes so that good things happen to you faster and faster. It might happen so fast that it's hard to keep track of. Eventually, you will just let go of the doubt and instead have the expectation and trust fully integrated.

You see all these amazing things happening; sometimes, doubt will still occur. While writing this book, I faced new fears and self-doubt. The biggest fear was what those closest to me would think of the book. Writing the book was an opportunity to peel off new layers of ego and heal old wounds.

I was afraid to sign up for mentorship with any of "the big ones" because I didn't want to be accused of stealing material. Even though we all know this is universal knowledge, it was still a fear of mine. Another fear was that my words wouldn't be as good as a best-selling author. Boy, was I wrong?

One day, a commercial showed up, and I thought to myself: "I will never be this big or able to speak in such a way." The universe responded instantaneously: "Your path is not to be that way; your path is to be you because someone needs to hear it just the way you speak it. Just be you. You are enough". When I heard it the first time, I immediately wrote it down. I shared it with those closest to me, and then it had to land. I hardly wrote for two months until the words appeared again. This time, I wrote them on my bathroom mirror: "Someone needs to hear your story. Your words are more than good enough," and then I did inspire action and picked up the pen again and continued to write from the heart, with the intention of helping you heal old wounds, attract wealth and create the future that you want.

Life is a rollercoaster of growth, curiosity, path corrections, lessons learned, and new insight. By reading this book and doing the exercises, you have raised your energy and set so many balls rolling. If there is any doubt in your mind about what you are capable of, please listen to the universe:

" YOUR PATH IS TO BE YOU. JUST BE YOU. THE MEANING OF LIFE IS TO HAVE EXPERIENCES AND GROW. YOU ARE ENOUGH, AND YOU ARE WORTHY OF WEALTH AND ABUNDANCE".

Epilogue

While writing about cleaning out kitchen covers, I reflect upon two drawers in my bathroom. They needed to be cleaned out. They were clogged with old toothbrushes, hair bands that had lost their elasticity, and old makeup. It can be challenging for me to throw out stuff like old makeup because often, those pieces had connections to my mom, and it would be like throwing out a piece of her. So, these two drawers had been at the bottom of the list of things to do for so long. I am ending the chapter, and one of my kids comes in with a note that was taped to our front door. It was from the plumber telling us that we had to empty cabinets under the sink in the kitchen and bathroom so they could do a checkup of all the pipes. Needless to say, I had no choice but to start cleaning and organizing.

I love when the universe "forces" us to take steps we wish to take but have blockage against. Now, the two drawers are cleaned, and I can feel new energy flowing in.

There were many times throughout this writing process when I faced similar experiences, but the most challenging part about writing was getting the editorial feedback for further review.

The first time it kept me from writing in weeks. I knew there was some good stuff in the feedback, and I knew that the book became better after editing, but it would still trigger the little girl in me who struggled in school. The little girl with a mild grade of dyslexia would wonder if she was not good enough. Initially, I would carry it inside, but eventually, I turned to some author friends to cry out. I learned that this is a normal feeling and that they go through the same thing even after publishing 10-15 books. I would return to the writing on my bathroom mirror: "Your words are good enough, and someone needs to hear it in just the way you express it."

I so often talk about how we become better by surrounding ourselves with people who are different from us. People who can challenge the way we think. I never said that it was the easiest step but, in the end, the result is so much better. When we solve challenges with different perspectives amazing stuff occurs. The same goes for facing new insecurities; the process can be extremely hard, but it is worth it in the end.

I REEVALUATE AND REFRAME MY STRUGGLES AS VALUABLE LESSONS AND THANK THE UNIVERSE FOR THEM, AS THEY HAVE MADE ME WHO I AM TODAY: HAPPY, HEALTHY, AND RICH.

Energy is an exchange

This is an energy exchange. I help you, and you help me. If there was any advice or insight in the book that helped you, inspired you, or changed your day for the better, please go to Amazon or your audiobook platform and rate this book with the best ratting that is possible for you to give.

Let's continue to exchange energy. You can find me on:

Webb: www.mettehaa.com
Blogg: http://adesiretoinspire.se/
Instagram: https://www.instagram.com/metteh_adesiretoinspire/

Thanks

I thank my followers for their unconditional love and guidance when I have asked for advice.

Thanks to my sister and friends for cheering me along. I especially thank Hanna, Titti, Catarina, and Anne-Mette for all your loving support and sound advice - Titti, especially, thanks for all the editorial feedback. You make me a better writer.

Thanks to my dad and uncle for allowing me to be me, answering my questions, and helping me heal my past. Thanks to my mom for all the good times.

Thanks, Susan and Camilla for being a shoulder to cry on. Thanks for being fabulous authors and willing to share your knowledge. Camilla thanks for the extra editing and good advice.

Thanks to Helena, Miljonarmamman, for sharing your valuable lessons and letting me into your life. Thanks for being brave and changing the lives of so many around you.

Thank to Max for allowing me into the studio six months before becoming a customer, just so I could feel and sense the energy of being in a studio.

Thanks to Joshua Sprague, Amanda Frances, and Cara Alwill for your different writing courses. Joshua, you helped me overcome my first fears and get my structure down on paper. You were my daily companion for 14 days in Italy and the month after that until I got in the way of myself. Amanda and Cara, thanks for picking me up from my short moment of self-doubt and getting me back into inspired action. I will forever be grateful for the knowledge the three of you have shared with me.

Thanks to Lisa and Josefine for co-creating some of the Miracle Calendars. Lisa without you there wouldn't have been a calendar, so thank you for trusting me. Josefine, thank you for challenging me on words and perspectives, it has truly been a part of making the calendar better.

I thank my kids for sleeping long in the mornings during summer, giving me the most precious time to start the writing process.

Thanks to my future partner for not showing up during this process, allowing me to give my time unconditionally to my second lover, source creator. Source creator, thank you for being with me during this process.

♥